Stories
of the World We Live In
Unpacking Global Issues from Leading Newspapers

Kyoko Horie

Harumi Go

Geoffrey Tozer

KINSEIDO

Kinseido Publishing Co., Ltd.
3-21 Kanda Jimbo-cho, Chiyoda-ku,
Tokyo 101-0051, Japan

First published 2024 by Kinseido Publishing Co., Ltd.

Design: DAITECH co., ltd.
Illustrations: Sayaka Ohara

はじめに

　本書は大学生が米英のクオリティペーパー（高級紙）記事を通して質の高い英語に触れ、一つ上のレベルの読解力を養い、さらにはさまざまなトピックについて自分の意見を表現することを目的として作成したものです。

　リーディングの活動には、読む前のスキーマ（背景知識）活性化や準備、文章を読む作業、読後の理解度確認の3段階があります。本書は、各段階にじっくり取り組むための多彩な練習問題を掲載しており、難易度の高い英文記事を読み解くリーディング力を着実に身に付けられる構成になっています。また、本文を読み終えた後、記事のテーマについての多種多様な意見の例を参考に、最終的には自分の意見を書く、といった発信する力を伸ばす練習を備えていることも本書の特徴です。

　全体を構成する6つの動詞カテゴリー（COMMUNICATE / WORK / DIVERSIFY / SURVIVE / SUSTAIN / INNOVATE）は、記事が扱うテーマが今現在も「動いている、変化している」事象であることを象徴しています。そして、この躍動する世界で起こる一つ一つの出来事や問題の奥には、関わる人々が織りなす無数の「ストーリー（物語）」が存在しています。本書はそのような個人の経験や視点から書かれた記事を多く選定することで、読み手が同じ人間として共感し、扱われている普遍的なテーマを身近な問題として考えやすくなることを目指しました。本書を読むことが、学生の皆さんにとって英語学習の枠を超えて、世界の問題を自分事として捉え深く考えるきっかけになることを願っております。

　最後になりましたが、本書の刊行にあたってご尽力いただいた四條雪菜氏、長島吉成氏、蔦原美智氏をはじめ、金星堂の皆様に心より感謝の意を表します。

著者一同

本書の使い方

導入文

記事のテーマに関連する設問に答える形で本文に入る準備をします。読む前に既に持っている知識や意見をクラスメートと話し合うのもよいでしょう。この時点で具体的にどのような内容がこれから読む記事に含まれるかを予測すること（Prediction）も大切です。

Vocabulary Sorting

読解のカギとなる単語や表現を4つのカテゴリー（関連語や同義語）に分類します。単語や表現の意味を調べる際は英英辞書を活用して語句のニュアンスを理解することもよいでしょう。ペアで話し合う際には、意味を調べるだけでなく、発音も確認し互いに声に出して言ってみましょう。

Words in Context

Vocabulary Sortingの語句を文中で使う練習です。この短いパッセージはこれから読む本文に関連する内容のため、調べた単語が実際にどのような文脈で使われるのか予測しやすくなります。語句を入れ終えたら、CD音声で解答とともに発音を確認し、全体を一度音読するのもよいでしょう。

Reading the Article

本文は1,000語前後の記事です。長文読解のポイントとしては、はじめに大まかなトピックや全体の流れを把握するために一読します。その際に分からない語句があっても逐一辞書で調べず、文脈から推測しながら読み進めます。全体像がつかめたら、今度は詳細を理解するために必要であれば単語などを調べながら2回目、3回目と精読します。特に、本書で取り上げるようなノンフィクションの内容については、登場人物同士の関係性を整理しながら読むことも大切です。また、*Notes*に挙げた記事の背景知識や追加情報も参考にして理解を深めましょう。

True or False

問題文が本文の内容に一致しているか否かを判断します。同じ内容が別の言葉で表現されているか、似て非なる内容になっているか、ありそうで書いていないかなどを判断するために本文に戻ってじっくり読み直すことが必要です。

Question & Answer

本文に関する設問に文章で答えます。そのまま抜き出せる短い答えもありますが、長い文になる場合は自分の言葉で簡潔にまとめるなどしてパラフレーズすることも心がけましょう。

Correction & Listening

要約文に含まれている文法上の誤りを見つけ訂正します。単数／複数、時制、品詞など細かい部分の間違いを見落とさないように、一文一文の構造を丁寧に見ていきましょう。終わったらCD音声で解答の確認をしますが、正しい答えを聞き取れないと答え合わせにならないので同時にリスニング練習にもなります。CD音声を聞きながら、要約文を声に出して読み上げ、本文の主旨を頭に入れましょう。

Reflecting on the Whole Article
Group Work

英文読解は単語や文章の意味を正確に理解することが重視されがちですが、記事全体の構成を知り、全体像をつかむことも同じくらい大切です。各段落グループのキーとなる英文を読んで、感じたことをペアまたはグループで話し合い、設問に答えながら内容を振り返りましょう。

Discussing the Issues
Posting Your Comment

英文記事を読みっぱなしにするのではなく、自分の意見をアウトプットする練習です。オンライン記事へのコメント投稿を模した例には色々な視点や立場の人の考えが述べられています。自分がどの意見に賛成、反対、共感するか、または全く違う意見を持つのかなど、できるだけ説得力のある理由や例で自分の意見を文章にまとめます。各コメントを参考に、クラスメートとディスカッションできることを目指しましょう。

Window to Further Research

記事を読んでテーマに興味を持ち、より深く知りたいと思った人のための参考図書リストです。同じテーマについて他の著者の視点や文章を読むことで、さらに視野を広げることができるでしょう。

Table of Contents

はじめに
本書の使い方

Stories
of The World We Live In

I

COMMUNICATE

Chapter 1

No Phones, No Apps, No Likes

The New York Times

What rules should people have about how, how much, and where to use a smartphone or other digital devices so it does not take over their lives?

V ocabulary S orting

次の語句をカテゴリーに分類しましょう。未知語はペアで意味を確認しましょう。

scroll	devout	frown on	selfie
post	bond	consumed	riot
burn out	app	distressed	hand-wringing
tear apart	classist		

Social media	Attachment / Connection	Critical reaction	Troubled condition (worry, pain, exhaustion)
•	•	•	•
•	•	•	•
•	•	•	•
•			•

W ords in C ontext

日本語のヒントを参考に、上の語句から適切な表現を選び、必要な場合は文に合うように形を変えて空欄に記入しましょう。　　○ CD1-02

Most people appreciate their smartphones. They can watch inspiring videos from their favorite influencers, or **1.** _____ with friends by **2.** _____ photos or messages

つながる　　　　　　　　　　　　　投稿する
online. However, some people are so **3.** _____ by social media that they get

夢中になる
addicted and this can cause **4.** _____. Another issue is the Orwellian notion that

苦悩
companies and governments may be monitoring our behavior through our smartphones.
5. _____ users need to consider both the convenience and risk of using smartphones.

信心深い

Reading the Article

CD1-03

'Luddite' teens don't want your likes

1 On a brisk recent Sunday, a band of teenagers met on the steps of Central Library on Grand Army Plaza in Brooklyn to start the weekly meeting of the Luddite Club, a high school group that promotes a lifestyle of self-liberation from social media and technology. As the dozen teens headed into Prospect Park, they hid away their iPhones — or, in the
5 case of the most devout members, their flip phones.

2 They marched up a hill toward their usual spot, a dirt mound located far from the park's crowds. Among them was Odille Zexter-Kaiser, a senior at Edward R. Murrow High School in Midwood. "It's a little frowned on if someone doesn't show up," Odille said. "We're here every Sunday, rain or shine, even snow. We don't keep in touch with each
10 other, so you have to show up."

3 After the club members gathered logs to form a circle, they sat and withdrew into a bubble of serenity. Some drew in sketchbooks. Others painted with a watercolor kit. One of them closed their eyes to listen to the wind. Many read intently.

4 "Lots of us have read this book called *Into the Wild*," said Lola Shub, a senior at Essex

¹⁵ Street Academy, referring to Jon Krakauer's 1996 nonfiction book about the nomad Chris McCandless, who died while trying to live off the land in the Alaskan wilderness. "We've all got this theory that we're not just meant to be confined to buildings and work. And that guy was experiencing life. Real life. Social media and phones are not real life."

5 "When I got my flip phone, things instantly changed," Lola continued. "I started using ²⁰ my brain. It made me observe myself as a person."

CD1-04

6 Briefly, the club members discussed how the spreading of their Luddite gospel was going. Founded last year by another Murrow High School student, Logan Lane, the club is named after Ned Ludd, the folkloric 18th-century English textile worker who supposedly smashed up a mechanized loom, inspiring others to take up his name and riot against ²⁵ industrialization.

7 A few days before the gathering, after the 3 p.m. dismissal at Murrow High School, a flood of students emerged from the building onto the street. Many of them were staring at their smartphones, but not Logan, the 17-year-old founder of the Luddite Club.

8 "We have trouble recruiting members," she said, "but we don't really mind it. All of us ³⁰ have bonded over this unique cause. To be in the Luddite Club, there's a level of being a misfit to it." She added: "But I wasn't always a Luddite, of course."

9 It all began during lockdown, she said, when her social media use took a troubling turn. "I became completely consumed," she said. "I couldn't not post a good picture if I had one. And I had this online personality of, 'I don't care,' but I actually did. I was definitely ³⁵ still watching everything." Eventually, too burned out to scroll past yet one more picture-perfect Instagram selfie, she deleted the app. "But that wasn't enough," she said. "So I put my phone in a box."

10 For the first time, she experienced life in the city as a teenager without an iPhone. She borrowed novels from the library and read them alone in the park. And she began waking ⁴⁰ up without an alarm clock at 7 a.m., no longer falling asleep to the glow of her phone at midnight.

11 While Logan's parents appreciated her metamorphosis, particularly that she was regularly coming home for dinner to recount her wanderings, they grew distressed that they couldn't check in on their daughter on a Friday night. Eventually, they insisted that ⁴⁵ she at least start carrying a flip phone.

12 "I still long to have no phone at all," she said. "My parents are so addicted. My mom got on Twitter, and I've seen it tear her apart. But I guess I also like it, because I get to feel a little superior to them."

CD1-05

13 At an all-ages punk show, she met a teen with a flip phone, and they bonded over their
50 worldview. "She was just a freshman, and I couldn't believe how well read she was," Logan said. "We walked in the park with apple cider and doughnuts and shared our Luddite experiences. That was the first meeting of the Luddite Club."

14 When school was back in session, Logan began preaching her evangel in the fluorescent-lit halls of Murrow. First she convinced Odille to go Luddite. Then Max. Then Clem. She
55 hung homemade posters recounting the tale of Ned Ludd onto corridors and classroom walls.

15 At a club fair, her enlistment table remained quiet all day, but little by little the group began to grow. Today, the club has about 25 members, and the Murrow branch convenes at the school each Tuesday. It welcomes students who have yet to give up their iPhones,
60 offering them the challenge of ignoring their devices for the hourlong meeting.

16 As Logan recounted the club's origin story over an almond croissant at the coffee shop, a new member, Julian, stopped in. Although he hadn't yet made the switch to a flip phone, he said he was already benefiting from the group's message. Then he ribbed Logan regarding a criticism one student had made about the club.

65 **17** "One kid said it's classist," he said. "I think the club's nice, because I get a break from my phone, but I get their point. Some of us need technology to be included in society. Some of us need a phone." "We get backlash," Logan replied. "The argument I've heard is we're a bunch of rich kids and expecting everyone to drop their phones is privileged."

18 With the end of her senior year in sight, and the pressures of adulthood looming, she
70 has also pondered what leaving high school might mean for her Luddite ways. "If now is the only time I get to do this in my life, then I'm going to make it count," she said. "But I really hope it won't end."

CD1-06

19 On a leafy street in Cobble Hill, she stepped into her family's townhouse, and she rushed upstairs to her room. The décor reflected her interests: There were stacks of books,
75 graffitied walls and, in addition to the sewing machine, a manual Royal typewriter and a Sony cassette player.

20 In the living room downstairs, her father, Seth Lane, an executive who works in I.T., offered thoughts on his daughter's journey. "I'm proud of her and what the club represents," he said. "But there's also the parent part of it, and we don't know where our kid is. You follow your kids now. You track them. It's a little Orwellian, I guess, but we're the helicopter parent generation. So when she got rid of the iPhone, that presented a problem for us, initially."

21 He'd heard about the Luddite Club's hand-wringing over questions of privilege. "Well, it's classist to make people need to have smartphones, too, right?" Mr. Lane said. "I think it's a great conversation they're having. There's no right answer."

1,172 words

By Alex Vadukul, Dec. 15, 2022, *The New York Times*

Notes

ℓ.7　Edward R. Murrow High School「エドワード・R・マロー高校」：
ニューヨーク州ブルックリンのミッドウッドにある公立の高校。1974年創立で、著名なジャーナリストでケネディ政権では広報・文化交流庁長官も務めたエドワード・R・マローに因んで命名された。芸術分野に力を入れているのが特色で、同校からはダーレン・アロノフスキー（映画監督）、ジャン＝ミシェル・バスキア（画家）、アダム・ヤウク（ラッパー、元ビースティボーイズ）など多くの芸術家を輩出している。

ℓ.14　*Into the Wild*『荒野へ』：
アメリカ人ジャーナリスト兼登山家のジョン・クラカワーが1996年に発表したノンフィクション。裕福な家庭に生まれながらも物質社会に疑問を抱き、大学卒業と同時に全財産を捨てアメリカ西部の荒野へと旅に出発、のちに餓死したクリス・マッカンドレスの生き様を自身の体験なども交えて綴り、ベストセラーとなった。2007年にはショーン・ペン監督で映画化もされている。

ℓ.23　Ned Ludd「ネッド・ラッド」：
イギリスの織工で、18世紀後半から19世紀初頭にかけて行われた産業革命に反対する機械破壊運動を主導したといわれる人物。この運動は彼に因んでLuddite movement（ラッダイト運動）と呼ばれ、機械化による失業の恐れや、粗悪品の量産などへの抗議として、これに賛同した労働者たちが自ら工場の機械を破壊した。現代ではLudditeという言葉は新しいテクノロジーへの反発（者）の意味で使われ、今回のLuddite Clubのほか、生成AIによる雇用機会や著作権の侵害に抵抗する際のキーワードとして見かけることも多くなった。

ℓ.80　Orwellian「オーウェル風の、オーウェルの小説のような」：
イギリスの作家ジョージ・オーウェルが1949年に発表した『1984年』（*Nineteen Eighty-Four*）は思想や言論、行動や労働といったあらゆるものが監視・統制される世界を描いたディストピア小説の金字塔だが、この小説や彼の他の著作にも散見される全体主義的で自由のない社会体制や風潮をさすときに使われ、その後形容詞として定着した。

ℓ.80　helicopter parent「ヘリコプターペアレント」：
ヘリコプターが空から地上を監視するように、子どもの周囲を監視して何かと干渉する過保護な親をさす。この言葉は1980年代から使われていたが、2000年代に入ってベビーブーマー世代の子が大学に入り出した頃に、親からの苦情が大学側に増え始めたことからよく使われるようになった。

True or **F**alse 英文を読んで、本文と合致する場合は T を、合致しない場合は F を記入しましょう。

1. The Sunday gathering is a meeting where the Luddite Club members spend time freely without touching their phones or thinking about social media.　　　　[　　]

2. Logan Lane got tired of social media because she could not stop posting pictures online and had to act as if she had a different character.　　　　[　　]

3. Logan's parents praised and fully accepted her new way of living without a phone. [　　]

4. The club welcomes students who have not yet given up carrying their phones.　[　　]

5. Logan plans to get the most out of the Luddite ways while in high school and get back to the modern way of life as soon as she graduates.　　　　[　　]

Question & **A**nswer 次の質問に英文で答えましょう。

1. Give one example of how the members of the Luddite Club spend time at the gathering.

_____

2. What criticisms do the club members sometimes receive?

_____

3. How does Logan's father explain the parents' perspectives of their children abandoning phones?

_____

Correction & **L**istening 以下は5箇所の文法上の誤りを含んだ記事の要約文です。誤りを正しく直しましょう。その後、正しい音声を聞いて答えを確認しましょう。

 CD1-07

　　A group of high school students in Brooklyn called the Luddite Club meet weekly to promote a lifestyle free from social media and technology. They gather in a park, leaving their iPhones behind, and engage in activities like drawing, painting, and reading. The club was founded by Logan Lane, which became disillusioned with social media and decided to live out it. She recruited members and spread the club's message in her school. The club faces critically for being classist, but members believe in the benefits for disconnecting from technology. Logan's parents worried at first, but now appreciate her transformation.

Reflecting on the Whole Article

多くの人が四六時中スマホを手放せなくなっている現代において、とても身につまされる内容ではないだろうか。本記事ではクラブの創設者ローガンを主軸に、スマホやSNSから解放されること、それに対する同世代からの批判、親世代とのギャップなどが語られている。日曜日の集会やローガンの自宅の様子など、インタビュー中の情景が記事の中で細かく描写されており、小説のような没入感を味わうことができる。

 以下は記事全体の流れと、キーとなる英文です。ペアまたはグループを作り、これらの英文を読んで感じたことをシェアしましょう。その後、各メンバーで分担して次の質問について考え、答えを発表し合いましょう。

Paragraphs **1** — **5**

ブルックリンの高校生たちが始めた「ラッダイト・クラブ」とは?

"It's a little frowned on if someone doesn't show up"

(Odille Zexter-Kaiser, member of the Luddite Club)

Q Why is it frowned on when someone doesn't come to the club gathering?

Paragraphs **6** — **12**

創設者ローガン(17歳)の話〜SNS依存からスマホを手放したあとの生活まで〜

"I couldn't not post a good picture if I had one. And I had this online personality of, 'I don't care,' but I actually did. I was definitely still watching everything."

(Logan Lane)

Q After Logan stopped using her phone, what changes did she experience?

Paragraphs **13** — **18**

少しずつ増える会員、そして「特権階級」批判

"The argument I've heard is we're a bunch of rich kids and expecting everyone to drop their phones is privileged." (Logan Lane)

Q Why might it be privileged to get everyone to drop their phones?

Paragraphs **19** — **21**

ローガンの父の眼差し──世代ギャップと娘の活動への所感

" ... It's a little Orwellian, I guess, but we're the helicopter parent generation...."

(Seth Lane)

Q Give an example of what he considers 'a little Orwellian.'

Discussing the Issues

今や生活必需品のスマホを捨てた若者たちに対しては、いろいろな意見があるだろう。以下は、本章の記事に寄せられたコメントである。

Posting Your **C**omment　次のコメントを参考に、あなた自身の意見を書いてみましょう。

Instagram addict, *4 hours ago*
I read somewhere that most people tend to grab their cell phone within 5 minutes of waking up every morning. It's true for me, and I really need to start putting down my phone for at least an hour like these kids do.

Andrea, *3 hours ago*
I strongly agree with the "classist" criticism of the club. As if to prove it, all members seem to be rich, well-educated teens living in the city.

Geronimo, *15 minutes ago*
Logan's father also has a point. Tech giants (they're definitely privileged!) are trying to get everything done with smartphones or digital devices, regardless of whether it is convenient or not. Shouldn't there be a more moderate option than the Luddite Club?

You, *now*

Window to Further Research

10代の若者の約2割は、スマホ閲覧に1日平均7時間を費やしているといわれ、学力の低下、睡眠や体力への悪影響などが懸念されている。しかし子どもの安全確認や災害時におけるスマホの必要性は否めない。そのうえで、どのような選択をするかは大きな課題であるが、以下はその選択に役立つであろう。

『スマホ脳』
　アンデシュ・ハンセン著、新潮社、2020年
長時間にわたるスマホ使用により引き起こされる睡眠障害、鬱、記憶力や集中力、学力の低下、依存症などの脳障害について解説し、デジタル時代へのアドバイスを提言している。

Stolen Focus: Why You Can't Pay Attention— and How to Think Deeply Again
　by Johann Hari, Crown, 2022
年々低下する現代人の集中力。著者は世界中の専門家に取材をし、集中力低下の原因が自分ではなく、外部の要因に「盗まれた（stolen）」のだという結論に至った。その12の要因を解き明かし、盗まれた集中力を取り戻す術を学ぶ。

Chapter
2

Disappearing Languages

National Geographic

If the population of a species drops too low, the danger of extinction increases. How about languages? How many speakers of a language are necessary to keep it alive?

V ocabulary S orting

次の語句をカテゴリーに分類しましょう。未知語はペアで意味を確認しましょう。

film	discuss	dwindling	suppression
track	banter	reminisce	document
persecution	archive	coercion	predicted to disappear
annex	go extinct	chatter	on the brink of extinction

Controlling act	Recording	Declining	Conversation
•	•	•	•
•	•	•	•
•	•	•	•
•	•	•	•

W ords in C ontext

日本語のヒントを参考に、上の語句から適切な表現を選び、必要な場合は文に合うように形を変えて空欄に記入しましょう。　　　　　◉ CD1-08

In a typical classroom, students exchange **1.** _____ as they enter the room, but
冗談のやり取り
once the class starts, they begin to **2.** _____ serious issues. Sometimes, the teacher
議論する
3. _____ about the old days. During the Covid 19 pandemic, it was not
思い出話をする
clear whether classes could continue, but teachers and students quickly got used to online
learning. Unfortunately, the usual **4.** _____ **5.** _____ as students appeared
おしゃべり　　　　　　　次第に減少した
in small boxes on computer screens. This was a good example of how language can either be
active or **6.** _____ depending on how people use it.
抑圧された

Reading the Article

 CD1-09

The race to save the world's disappearing languages

1 On a residential block at the border between Brooklyn and Queens, Gottscheer Hall appears like a mirage from 1945.

2 Blue awnings advertise the space for weddings and events. Inside, an entryway is covered with the saccharine smiles of "Miss Gottschee" contestants from decades past. "Back then you had to know the language to compete," says 92-year-old Alfred Belay, pointing out his daughter's beaming face from the 1980s. Nowadays, there are years with only a single contestant in the pageant.

3 Belay has been coming to Gottscheer Hall since he arrived in America more than 60 years ago. Then, the neighborhood was filled with refugees from Gottschee, a settlement that once occupied the highlands of modern-day Slovenia. Now, he's one of a few thousand remaining speakers of its language, Gottscheerisch. Every Christmas he leads a service in his 600-year-old native language that few understand. "Imagine if someone who plays music suddenly can't use their fingers," he says. "We're still alive but can only remember these things."

4 Belay and his sister, 83-year-old Martha Hutter, have agreed to let 26-year-old Daniel Bogre Udell film them having a conversation. They walk past the dark wood bar of Gottscheer Hall serving pretzels and sausages, and they climb the stairs to an empty banquet room. Bogre Udell sets up his camera and the siblings begin to banter in their inscrutable Germanic mother tongue.

◉ CD1-10

5 Hearing such a rare language spoken on a residential block of Queens is not unusual for Bogre Udell, the co-founder of a nonprofit called Wikitongues. There are some 800 languages spoken within the 10-mile radius of New York City, which is more than 10 percent of the world's estimated 7,099 languages. Since he has decided to record all of them, the melting-pot metropolis is a natural launching point.

6 Bogre Udell, who speaks four languages, met Frederico Andrade, who speaks five, at the Parsons New School in New York City. In 2014, they launched an ambitious project to make the first public archive of every language in the world. They've already documented more than 350 languages, which they are tracking online, and plan to hit 1,000 in the coming years.

7 "When humanity loses a language, we also lose the potential for greater diversity in art, music, literature, and oral traditions," says Bogre Udell. "Would Cervantes have written the same stories had he been forced to write in a language other than Spanish? Would the music of Beyoncé be the same in a language other than English?"

8 Between 1950 and 2010, 230 languages went extinct, according to the UNESCO *Atlas of the World's Languages in Danger*. Today, a third of the world's languages have fewer than 1,000 speakers left. Every two weeks a language dies with its last speaker; 50 to 90 percent of them are predicted to disappear by the next century.

9 In rare cases, political will and a thorough written record can resurrect a lost language. Hebrew was extinct from the fourth century BC to the 1800s, and Catalan only bloomed during a government transition in the 1970s. In 2001, more than 40 years after the last native speaker died, the language of Oklahoma's Miami tribe started being learned by students at Miami University in Ohio. The internet has connected rare language speakers with each other and with researchers. Even texting has helped formalize languages that don't have a set writing system.

◉ CD1-11

10 Knowing they wouldn't be able to record, or even locate, the majority of these languages themselves, Wikitongues has enlisted a network of volunteers in 40 countries to film native speakers talking in the past, present, and future tenses of their mother tongue. To get a range of tones and emotions, they're asked to reminisce about childhood, talk about romance, and discuss their hopes and goals.

11 One volunteer in the South Pacific islands of Vanuatu recorded a language that had never before been studied by linguists. Another tracked down a speaker of Ainu, a rare indigenous language in Japan that is an "isolate," meaning it bears no relation to any other known language.

12 Priceless documentation opportunities disappear regularly. Not long ago, one of the last two speakers of a Saami language dialect in the Russian steppes died right before his recording session with Wikitongues. Some 500 languages could slip through their grasp in the next five years, they estimate.

13 Political persecution, a lack of preservation, and globalization are to blame for the dwindling language diversity. For much of the 20th century, governments across the world have imposed language on indigenous people, often through coercion. Some 100 aboriginal languages in Australia have disappeared since European settlers arrived. A half-century after China annexed Tibet, dozens of distinct dialects with unique alphabets are on the verge of extinction. Studies have shown that suppressing language impairs everything from health to school performance.

14 This forced suppression, however, is no longer the biggest threat facing our linguistic ecosystem. "Most languages die today not because of abject and outright persecution — though this does happen on occasion — but rather because they are made unviable," says Andrade. Factors like climate change and urbanization force linguistically diverse rural and coastal communities to migrate and assimilate to new communities with new languages. "This form of language loss is a cancer, not a gunshot."

◎ CD1-12

15 In Gottscheer Hall, Belay and Hutter transform as they chatter for Daniel Bogre Udell's video camera. At one point Hutter breaks into song. In Gottscheerisch, they recall growing up in a single bedroom home where they spoke Gottscheerisch — German was used for school and church.

16 In 1941, Gottschee was annexed by the Italians and its residents were sent to resettlement camps. Four years later, the Gottscheer Relief Association opened its doors to the thousands of immigrants arriving in New York. By the time Belay and Hutter arrived, in the 1950s, the neighborhood was so full of immigrants that Hutter was barely able to practice her English.

17 The newcomers spoke Gottscheerisch to each other and raised their kids with English. Now, 60 years later, Belay has started speaking to his kids in Gottscheerisch for the first time, but the language is on the brink of extinction.

18 As a street language, Gottscheerisch was rarely written down. It could only be learned by ear until 1994, when Hutter published a five-year effort collecting definitions for 1,400 words: the first English-Gottscheerisch dictionary.

19 "The old Gottscheers were convinced that nobody can learn Gottscheerisch, so they didn't try to teach it," Hutter recalls. "But any language can be learned, so I thought, 'This old language is going to die and they won't know anything.'" "We did the same thing," Belay interjects. "Our kids could have learned it."

20 "There is a time in the future when families won't speak it," says Hutter. "When they'll say, 'Our family spoke — *what was it?*'"

1,123 words

By Nina Strochlic, Apr. 17, 2018, *National Geographic*

Notes

ℓ.4　Gottschee「コチェーヴィエ（スロベニア語）、ゴットシェー（ドイツ語）」:
クルカ川とコルパ川の間に位置する、現スロベニアの市。スロベニアで最大の面積を誇る自然豊かな地域で、かつてはドイツ人のコミュニティであった。

ℓ.11　Gottscheerisch「ゴットシェー語」:
上記ドイツ人居住地区で20世紀前半まで主要言語の一つ。ゴットシェー語は口語として会話などで使われ、書き言葉としては標準ドイツ語が使われていた。19世紀に多くの話者がアメリカに移住したことや第二次世界大戦後にユーゴスラビア政府によって使用が禁止されたことなどから話者が激減し、現在消滅の危機に瀕している。

ℓ.21　Wikitongues「ウィキタングス」:
アメリカ・ニューヨーク州で、消えゆく言語の保護・存続を目的として活動するNPO団体。2014年設立。当団体のホームページには、消滅危機にある言語の基本情報や話者が話している姿を撮影した映像が公開されている。

ℓ.34　*Atlas of the World's Languages in Danger*『危機に瀕する世界言語の地図』:
国連教育科学文化機関（UNESCO）が消滅危機に瀕している世界の言語を包括的にまとめた書籍。世界の言語消滅の危険度に対して、話者の年齢層や言語の使用場面という観点から「Vulnerable」「Definitely endangered」「Severely endangered」「Critically endangered」「Extinct」の5つのカテゴリーに分けて評価している。

True or **F**alse | 英文を読んで、本文と合致する場合は T を、合致しない場合は F を記入しましょう。

1. Bogre Udell, the founder of Wikitongues, began his recording project from New York City, which is a melting pot of rare languages. [   ]

2. Hebrew went extinct in the 1970s. [   ]

3. Wikitongues asks speakers who appear in the film to talk solely in formal expressions.

   [   ]

4. Precious opportunities to record rare languages can disappear suddenly because of the death of the speakers. [   ]

5. Belay raised his children with his native language. [   ]

Question & **A**nswer | 次の質問に英文で答えましょう。

1. What project did Bogre Udell start in 2014?

   _____

2. According to Bogre Udell, why is saving languages important for humanity?

   _____

3. What is the main cause of languages disappearing in the 20th century?

   _____

Correction & **L**istening | 以下は5箇所の文法上の誤りを含んだ記事の要約文です。誤りを正しく直しましょう。その後、正しい音声を聞いて答えを確認しましょう。

 CD1-13

　　Gottscheerisch is in the brink of extinction, so it is important to document it. A nonprofit organization called Wikitongues have been working on this. By filming a range for native speakers' conversation, they have documented and made an online archive of more than 350 languages, hoping to save them from disappearing. Today, it is said that a three of the world's languages have fewest than 1,000 speakers. Decades ago, many languages faced crisis due to political coercion. Now, however, factors like climate change and urbanization are the biggest threats making languages unviable.

Reflecting on the Whole Article

本記事はアメリカへ渡ったドイツ系移民の言葉、ゴットシェー語の保護活動を軸に、他の消えゆく言語の例も交えながら消滅する原因を学術的に考察している。言語を後世に残そうとする前向きな取り組みと、ゴットシェー語の危機的な状況を説明した話者たちのリアルな言葉のコントラストが丁寧にまとめられており、この問題について考える余白を残している。

 以下は記事全体の流れと、キーとなる英文です。ペアまたはグループを作り、これらの英文を読んで感じたことをシェアしましょう。その後、各メンバーで分担して次の質問について考え、答えを発表し合いましょう。

Paragraphs **1** — **4**

600年の歴史を誇る言語「ゴットシェー語」の危機

"Imagine if someone who plays music suddenly can't use their fingers" (Alfred Belay)

Q What does Belay mean by this comment in the context of language?

Paragraphs **5** — **9**

消えゆく言語を救うWikitonguesの壮大な計画、世界の消滅危機言語の今

Hearing such a rare language spoken on a residential block of Queens is not unusual for Bogre Udell, the co-founder of a nonprofit called Wikitongues.

Q Why is it not unusual to hear rare languages in this area?

Paragraphs **10** — **14**

Wikitongues保護活動の実際、言語が消滅する原因

"This form of language loss is a cancer, not a gunshot." (Frederico Andrade)

Q What do you think Andrade means by this?

Paragraphs **15** — **20**

消滅の一途をたどるゴットシェー語の歴史と厳しい現状

"There is a time in the future when families won't speak it," says Hutter. "When they'll say, 'Our family spoke — what was it?'"

Q Why is Hutter so pessimistic about the future of Gottscheerisch?

Discussing the Issues

消えゆく言語を保護できるのか——。本記事に登場する消滅言語のさまざまな原因をふまえながら考えてみよう。以下は、本章の記事に寄せられたコメントである。

Posting Your Comment
次のコメントを参考に、あなた自身の意見を書いてみましょう。

Londoner, *8 hours ago*
As the article suggested, minority languages are becoming unviable. We can't swim against the tide forever. It's time we embraced English as a universal language rather than spending so much time and money on languages that are certain to disappear.

Alice, *just now*
I'm an elementary school teacher in Kwethluk, Alaska. We are teaching our Yupik language at school. English is taught in the morning and Yupik in the afternoon. Unfortunately, this dual program is getting harder to teach, as parents, especially young parents, speak to their children in English at home. We are losing our language and culture.

You, *now*
_____
_____
_____

Window to Further Research

2週間に一つの言語が消失しているといわれる現代。言語の消滅が意味するものとは何か、そして消滅の危機からその言語を保護するためには何ができるだろうか。以下はケーススタディとともに考察するための参考図書である。

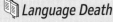 *Language Death*
by David Crystal, Cambridge University Press, 2014
言語の消滅は今に始まったことではないが、さまざまな要因が絡み、近年その勢いを増している。言語の消滅は「人類の知的遺産の喪失」と定義する筆者が、言語消滅の問題を考える意義や消滅の原因、そして消滅言語をいかに守っていくかを提唱する。

 A Death in the Rainforest: How a Language and a Way of Life Came to an End in Papua New Guinea
by Don Kulick, Algonquin Books, 2019
自らの言語を「話さない」という選択をした、パプアニューギニアのある村。30年間にわたって寝食を共にしながら、言語の消失について調査をした言語人類学者によるルポルタージュ。

Can We Communicate with Animals?

The New Yorker

Animals make noises and seem to communicate with each other, but at what level do they communicate? Is it possible for people to understand their thoughts and emotions?

V_{ocabulary} S_{orting}

次の語句をカテゴリーに分類しましょう。未知語はペアで意味を確認しましょう。

perceive	decode	converse	ultrasonic
whistle	vocalize	pod	gesture
cetacean	acknowledge	decipher	understanding
cognitive	large body of data	articulate	

Dolphin	Analysis	Expression	Comprehension
•	•	•	•
•	•	•	•
•	•	•	•
•		•	•

W_{ords in} C_{ontext}

日本語のヒントを参考に、上の語句から適切な表現を選び、必要な場合は文に合うように形を変えて空欄に記入しましょう。　　◎ CD1-14

Dolphins, classified as **1.** _____, live together in **2.** _____ and
　　　　　　　　　　　　　　　　　海洋哺乳類　　　　　　　　　　　　　　　　　　　　　群れ
communicate through clicks and **3.** _____, often in an **4.** _____ range
　　　　　　　　　　　　　　　　　　　　　　　　　　口笛　　　　　　　　　　　　　　　　　超音波
that humans cannot hear. Researchers are able to decode some of these signals with the help

of A.I. They have also taught dolphins sounds, which the animals have assimilated into their

lexicon. Because we think so differently from dolphins, however, some people think it is

difficult to fully **5.** _____ their world.
　　　　　　　　　　　　　　理解する

Reading the Article

 CD1-15

The challenges of animal translation

1 Disney's 2019 remake of its 1994 classic "The Lion King" was a box-office success. But it was also, in some ways, a failed experiment. The film's photo-realistic, computer-generated animals spoke with the rich, complex voices of actors — and many viewers found it hard to reconcile the complex intonations of those voices with the feline gazes on the screen.
5 In giving such persuasively nonhuman animals human personalities and thoughts, the film created a kind of cognitive dissonance. Disney's filmmakers had stumbled onto the gap between animal minds and our own.

2 Many animal lovers look upon the prospect of communication between animals and humans with hope: they think that, if only we could converse with other creatures, we
10 might be inspired to protect and conserve them properly. But others warn that, whenever we attempt to communicate with animals, we risk projecting our ideas and preconceptions

onto them. We might do this simply through the act of translation: any human language constrains the repertoire of things that can be said, or perhaps even thought, for those using it.

15 **3** Today, animal-translation technologies are being developed that use the same "machine learning" approach that is applied to human languages in services such as Google Translate. These systems use neural networks to analyze vast numbers of example sentences, inferring from them general principles of grammar and usage, and then apply those patterns in order to translate sentences the system has never seen. Denise Herzing, the founder and research
20 director of the nonprofit Wild Dolphin Project, is now using similar algorithms, coupled with underwater keyboards and computers, to try to decode dolphin communications. "It may be that our mobile technology will be the same technology that helps us communicate with another species," Herzing said in a 2013 TED talk.

CD1-16

4 But other researchers doubt that genuine translation can be easily achieved between
25 species that don't share the same basic perceptual and cognitive processes. For example, Con Slobodchikoff, an animal behavorist, said, "Bees and some birds see in the ultraviolet range of the visual spectrum, but we don't. Bats, dolphins, dogs, and cats hear sounds in the ultrasonic range, but we don't." Although Slobodchikoff insists that animals "have language, perceive time, have emotions, think, and plan," he also argues that "each animal
30 species has key differences that make it unique." We are as distinct as we are alike.

5 Those differences are dictated by many factors, including physiology and brain structure, the nature of the animal's environment, and the kinds of experience that environment supplies. The resulting divergences can be daunting. The last shared ancestor of humans and dolphins, for instance, lived an estimated ninety-five million years ago. Today, many
35 dolphins might as well live on a different planet — a gravity-free world that's typically blue-green in all directions, with no shadows or smells. What concepts are needed to navigate such a place? Whatever they may be, dolphins communicate them through sequences of whistles made by nasal-tissue vibration, which many dolphin researchers see as a proto-language — what you might jokingly call "dolphish." "Dolphins vocalize
40 profusely when they're all together, and the vocalizations are extremely complex," Marcelo Magnasco, a dolphin researcher, said. "They appear to be conversing with one another." Each dolphin in a pod has a signature whistle; dolphins use these whistles to summon one another, and to tell other members of their pod where they are if they lose visual contact.

6 This much we know. But Magnasco doesn't think that anyone has achieved a basic understanding of dolphish. "I'm not yet confident that I know what is the signal, what is the variation, what is the intention," he said. "You need an extremely large body of data to do that, and it's unclear that we have enough yet."

CD1-17

7 Still, there are hints that it might be possible. In 2013, Herzing and her team at the Wild Dolphin Project used a machine-learning algorithm called Cetacean Hearing and Telemetry (CHAT), designed to identify meaningful signals in dolphin whistles. The algorithm picked out a sound within a dolphin pod that the researchers had earlier trained the dolphins to associate with sargassum seaweed — a clumpy, floaty plant that dolphins sometimes play with. The dolphins may have assimilated the new "word," and begun using it in the wild.

8 Moreover, between 2016 and 2019, marine-mammal scientist Diana Reiss and Magnasco collaborated on studies that used an eight-foot underwater touch screen fitted with dolphin-friendly interactive apps, including a version of Whack-A-Mole in which fish move across the display. Using such systems, it's possible to ask animals about their preferences among two or more alternatives — the same approach that child psychologists often take in trying to understand the reasoning of preverbal infants. Roger Payne, a whale-song expert, has explained how groups of alternatives might be used to pose ever-more-specific inquiries. "We might try asking dolphins direct questions," he said. "Do dolphins fear boats? Are sharks scary? Which of the following sharks is most scary?"

9 The challenge, of course, is that it's humans posing the questions and determining the choice of answers. But that's changing. "The exciting thing about artificial intelligence and computer technology is that we are beginning to be able to decipher animal languages and animal cognition on terms that are meaningful to the animals, and not on our terms," Slobodchikoff told me. Today's machine-learning systems analyze data and look for correlations with startling efficiency; often, they find statistical connections that human analysts miss. Given enough training data, these A.I. algorithms can also extract semantic meaning from a range of non-linguistic inputs.

10 In theory, a machine-learning system is particularly well suited to the problem of translating animalese. The loose correspondences between human and animal words and concepts may not matter to an A.I.; neither will the fact that animal ideas may be expressed not as vocalizations but as gestures, sequences of movements, or changes in skin texture. A neural network makes no assumptions about the nature of the input data; as long as there is some aspect of an animal's behavioral repertoire that represents or expresses something that our languages can also express, the algorithm has a chance of spotting it.

11 If we could speak to them, dolphins wouldn't understand the metaphor of a glass being half full or half empty. But how much does that matter? We can be discouraged by the fact
80 that concepts that are universal among humans have no place in the conceptual landscape of the dolphin; alternatively, we can be encouraged by the possibility that there might be any overlap at all. It's incredible to think that people and dolphins might communicate about anything, even seaweed. It may be that the most interesting, revealing part of dolphish is precisely the part that lies outside our own lexicon — which is to say, outside
85 our own minds. If, in fact, we find ourselves unable to fully reconstruct another creature's mental world, it may be enough just to acknowledge the reality of what we can't articulate.

1,151 words

By Philip Ball, Apr. 27, 2021, *The New Yorker*

Notes

ℓ.1 Disney's 2019 remake of its 1994 classic "The Lion King":
1994年の名作アニメーション映画『ライオンキング』が四半世紀を経て、同じディズニーでフルCGでリメイクされた。キャストはドナルド・グローバー、ビヨンセ・ノウルズなど。本文にあるように興行的には成功し、同年の世界興行ランキング第2位を記録した。しかし、あまりにも擬人化された動物のCGに、一部の観客や批評家からは違和感や恐怖感を持たれ、実際の野生動物の世界から著しく乖離してしまったことを嘆く意見が出るなど、賛否が分かれる結果となった。

ℓ.16 Google Translate「グーグル翻訳」:
2006年にGoogle社が提供を開始した翻訳アプリ・サイト。同社のブラウザGoogle Chromeではあらかじめ統合されており、2022年時点で130以上の言語を翻訳することができる。2016年に、人間の脳機能を模倣して作られたシステムであるニューラルネットワーク(Neural Network)を導入し、翻訳の精度が飛躍的に向上した。

ℓ.20 Wild Dolphin Project「ワイルド・ドルフィン・プロジェクト」:
主にタイセイヨウマダライルカ(Stenella frontalis)の特定の群れについて研究する非営利の研究団体。1985年にデニーズ・ハージングによって設立された。研究の内容は、イルカの行動、社会構造、コミュニケーション、生息域など多岐に及ぶ。本文で紹介されたAI技術を使ったイルカの鳴き声の解読はジョージア工科大学との共同プロジェクトとして2023年現在も進行中。

ℓ.23 TED talk「TEDトーク」:
1984年設立の非営利団体TED(Technology Entertainment Design)が主催する会議(TED Conference)は2006年よりインターネットを通じて動画配信されるようになった。これがTED Talksで、さまざまな分野から著名な人物を招いて開催されている。これまでにビル・ゲイツやU2のボノ、ビル・クリントンなど錚々たる顔ぶれが登壇している。

ℓ.56 Whack-A-Mole「モグラたたきゲーム」:
ライスとマグナスコによる研究チームのプロジェクトでは、バーチャルな魚が泳ぐのをスクリーンに写し出し、それを見たイルカがタッチすると魚が消えるという仕組みを作った。10歳のイルカで試してみると、すぐに仕組みを理解し、スクリーン前でピタッと止まり、魚にタッチし始めたという。

True or **F**alse | 英文を読んで、本文と合致する場合は T を、合致しない場合は F を記入しましょう。

1. Many viewers of "The Lion King" felt that the human voices given to the nonhuman characters did not match well. [   ]

2. We tend to assume that animals share the same ideas that humans have. [   ]

3. Dolphins use complex vocalizations to send various signals to other dolphins. [   ]

4. The experiment by Wild Dolphin Project using Cetacean Hearing and Telemetry revealed that teaching new words to dolphins was not possible. [   ]

5. A.I. can spot semantic meaning from a range of inputs, including gestures. [   ]

Question & **A**nswer | 次の質問に英文で答えましょう。

1. What is one benefit that animal lovers hope to derive from communication between animals and humans?

_____

2. Why do some researchers doubt that genuine translation of animal languages can be easily achieved?

_____

3. What is one merit of using today's machine-learning systems for animal translation?

_____

Correction & **L**istening | 以下は 5 箇所の文法上の誤りを含んだ記事の要約文です。誤りを正しく直しましょう。その後、正しい音声を聞いて答えを確認しましょう。

 CD1-19

In recent times, there's been a growing interest in communicating with animals in the hope that it may lead to best conservation efforts. Some researchers are using technology to translate animal languages. However, there are challenges in bridging the communication gap among humans and animals. Animals perceive the world different due to their unique senses and experiences, making it difficult for humans to understand its languages. We must acknowledge that certain concepts might be beyond our grasp. Still, the possibility of even limit communication with animals is fascinating and could offer valuable insights into their worlds.

Reflecting on the Whole Article

本記事は、動物と言葉を交わし、心の交流をはかりたいという多くの動物愛好家の夢が、テクノロジーの進化によって現実になり得る可能性とともに、山積する課題や懐疑的な考え方も紹介している。最終的には、簡単には解明できない研究分野だからこその面白さがあるという筆者の見解で締めくくられる。探究心を持つことの大切さを、今一度思い出させてくれる。

 以下は記事全体の流れと、キーとなる英文です。ペアまたはグループを作り、これらの英文を読んで感じたことをシェアしましょう。その後、各メンバーで分担して次の質問について考え、答えを発表し合いましょう。

Paragraphs 1 − 3

人間は動物と意思疎通を図れるのか？ーー動物翻訳の可能性

"It may be that our mobile technology will be the same technology that helps us communicate with another species" (Denise Herzing)

Q Explain how the mobile technology used by Denise Herzing works.

Paragraphs 4 − 6

動物翻訳への疑念ーー動物種によって異なる知覚・認知プロセス、イルカの例

... "each animal species has key differences that make it unique." (Con Slobodchikoff)

Q What are two unique features of animals that make genuine human-animal translation difficult?

Paragraphs 7 − 10

動物−人間のコミュニケーションへの道を開く複数のAIプロジェクト

The dolphins may have assimilated the new "word," and begun using it in the wild.

Q How did researchers know they had succeeded in introducing a new "word" into the dolphin's vocabulary, and how might this be expanded?

Paragraph 11

動物−人間のコミュニケーションに対する筆者の見解

If, in fact, we find ourselves unable to fully reconstruct another creature's mental world, it may be enough just to acknowledge the reality of what we can't articulate.

Q How might we be either discouraged or encouraged by our attempts to communicate with dolphins?

Discussing the Issues

人−動物の異種間コミュニケーションはやはり難しいのか、むしろ違うからこそ面白いのか、など自分なりにこのテーマに関して思いを巡らせてみよう。以下は、本章の記事に寄せられたコメントである。

 Posting Your **C**omment | 次のコメントを参考に、あなた自身の意見を書いてみましょう。

David, *5 hours ago*
I have a dog, and I wish I understood what she feels. I believe animal translation could lead to early detection of animal illnesses and help them to live with more comfort.

Angie, *4 hours ago*
It would be amazing to know what animals are trying to say, but I wonder if all these projects don't put too much stress on them.

Jessica, *2 hours ago*
Although we may never be able to communicate perfectly with animals, we should celebrate the rapid progress that we are making. With advanced technology, we may be able to improve animal welfare and create a society where animals can live safely.

You, *now*

_____

_____

_____

 Window to Further Research

近年の動物生態学の研究により、知られざる動物の生態がますます明らかになりつつある。動物実験、畜産業や野生動物の保護、ペット殺処分などの問題が注目されているのもそのためだろう。人間と動物の関係の再構築が求められている今、それについて考えを深めるには以下の文献がおすすめである。

 The Inner Life of Animals: Surprising Observations of a Hidden World
by Peter Wohlleben, Vintage, 2018
ドイツの「森林官」が、動物の生態や行動における研究や観察をもとに、喜びや哀しみ、感謝、恥といった感情や意識を人間だけではなく、動物や昆虫、植物に至るまでの多くの生き物が持ち合わせていると主張する。

 Animals in Translation
by Temple Grandin & Catherine Johnson, Mariner Books, 2006
自閉症の動物学者である著者は、自閉症の人間と動物の認識に共通点があり、健常者の思考回路こそが「ミステリー」だという。最新の動物学の研究結果から視点の転換の必要性を示唆している。

The Washington Post

Basic Information

創立	1877年
創業者	スティルソン・ハッチンス
形態	日刊紙
本社	アメリカ合衆国ワシントンD.C.
スローガン	民主主義は暗闇の中で死ぬ （Democracy Dies in Darkness）

ポスト（The Post）、ワポ（WaPo）の愛称で親しまれ、アメリカ本国、特にワシントンD.C.を中心とした連邦機関が集まるエリアでは最もよく読まれている高級紙である。外交・紛争など国際関係に強く、格調高い論説は国内外に大きな影響力をもつ。

それまで「セントルイス・タイムズ」を発行し、自身も記者をしていたスティルソン・ハッチンスがワシントンD.C.に移り、1877年に創刊。1880年には日曜版を加え、D.C.で最初の日刊紙（週7日発行の新聞）となった。その後所有者は転々とし、世界大恐慌後の1933年に破産し、競売にかけられた。同年、金融家のユージン・メイヤーが同紙を落札し新オーナーとなる。メイヤーは立て直しに尽力し、その後オーナーはメイヤーの女婿のフィル・グラハム、そしてグラハムの娘のキャサリン・グラハムへと移った。キャサリン・グラハムの下、編集長ベン・ブラッドリーの時代に同紙はウォーターゲート事件をはじめ数々の歴史的スクープを連発し、黄金期を迎えた。

現在は、アマゾン創業者のジェフ・ベゾスの個人投資会社ナッシュ・ホールディングスLLCの傘下となり、デジタル化へのシフトに重きを置いている。

大統領を辞任に追い込んだ「ウォーターゲート事件」

大統領選挙期間の最中の1972年6月、ワシントンD.C.のウォーターゲート・ビルにある民主党本部に不法侵入したとして5人の男が逮捕される。駆け出しのポスト記者ボブ・ウッドワードはこの裁判の取材中、容疑者の所持品に無線機や小型カメラがあったり、1人がCIAの警備官だったりと、この事件が単なる窃盗ではないことを確信する。そして先輩記者のカール・バーンスタインとともに深掘り取材を進めていくうちに、5人が共和党に雇われて盗聴器を仕掛けようとしたことが判明する。この事件を発端に当時のニクソン大統領は辞任に追い込まれた（大統領で任期中に辞任したのは初めてで、以降もない）。二人の記者の活躍はのちに『大統領の陰謀（原題：All the President's Men）』として映画化され、ウッドワードをロバート・レッドフォード、バーンスタインをダスティン・ホフマンが演じた。

Stories
of The World We Live In

II

WORK

Escape from Burnout

The New York Times

Have you ever felt like you were "burning out"? If so, when did you get that feeling? How did you cope with it?

Vocabulary **S**orting 次の語句をカテゴリーに分類しましょう。未知語はペアで意味を確認しましょう。

professor	dread	indifference	strain
patient	furious	trucker	journalist
physician	stoical	wage earner	breadwinner
suicidal	skeptic	put food on the table	

Occupation	Provide(r)	Stressful emotion	Attitude
•	•	•	•
•	•	•	•
•	•	•	•
•		•	•

Words in **C**ontext 日本語のヒントを参考に、上の語句から適切な表現を選び、必要な場合は文に合うように形を変えて空欄に記入しましょう。 ◎ CD1-20

Traditional male jobs include a **1.** _____ driving on the road and a (トラック運転手) **2.** _____ who treats the sick. Men have accepted their role as breadwinners (外科医) who **3.** _____ with a **4.** _____ attitude, rarely (家族を養う) (ストイックな) complaining. Losing this role can cause depression or even **5.** _____ thoughts. (自殺の) Nowadays, men can express their feelings more, but people still see men as providers. We have to be **6.** _____ as it takes time for society to change. (忍耐強い)

Reading the Article

CD1-21

How men burn out

1 Eight years ago, I had a great job as a tenured professor at a small college in Pennsylvania. I seemed to have it made: autonomy, security, excellent benefits, even a modicum of prestige. But then I started to dread going to work. The students' indifference to my teaching felt like a personal insult. I became furious in response to minor slights from colleagues and
5 got into heated arguments in faculty meetings. I was burning out.

2 When I came home, I complained on the phone to my wife, who was beginning her own academic career at a college 200 miles away. But her patient ear was not enough to solve the problem. Neither was a semester of unpaid leave while we lived on her salary. When I went back to work, my burnout picked up right where it left off. My wife ultimately
10 saved me when she was offered a job in Texas. I quit mine and followed her.

3 Despite my relief, I felt like a failure not only as an academic, but also as a man. Even as gender roles seem increasingly flexible and open to revision, we are still a society where men attempt to prove their manhood through their performance at work. And I couldn't do my job.

CD1-22

15 **4** The intense public discussion of burnout during the pandemic has given too little attention to how men experience this problem. Articles on mothers' burnout far outnumber ones on dads'. There is (rightly) much public concern about burnout among nurses but little focus on it among truckers.

5 Academics and journalists have good reason to concentrate on women. The "second 20 shift" of child care continues to put disproportionate strain on working mothers. And there is evidence that women burn out at higher rates than men. According to a national study published in 2019, female physicians were at 32 percent greater risk of burnout than their male colleagues.

6 That disparity is a problem, but in a profession where the burnout rate is 44 percent, 25 there are still hundreds of thousands of male doctors suffering and potentially putting patients in danger.

7 If we want to end burnout, we have to address the problem for men as well as women. And to address men's burnout in particular, we have to acknowledge that consciously or not, our society still largely equates masculinity with being a stoical wage earner. Not all 30 men view themselves this way, and even men who don't are still susceptible to burnout. But research shows that men and women tend to undergo burnout differently. The signature patterns in male burnout each reflect an enduring breadwinner ethos that does not serve men well.

8 The way men burn out as parents also reflects the way they are conditioned by the 35 breadwinner ethos. In one study, researchers in Belgium found that while mothers scored higher on the parental burnout measure, fathers more quickly exhibited burnout and its negative consequences: escape fantasies, suicidal ideation and neglect of children. That is, given the same level of parenting stress, fathers reacted much worse than mothers did, putting both themselves and their children at greater risk of harm.

40 **9** "Fathers may be more vulnerable to demands arising from a role which is gender-typed

and not seen as an integral part of being a man," the Belgian researchers write. A skeptic might see this as evidence that men are weak and coddled. The researchers, however, see it as a sign that societies need to do a better job of preparing men to share the burden of parenthood.

10 When men encounter problems at work or elsewhere in their lives, they are much less likely than women to talk about it, in either public or private. Written accounts of male burnout are hard to find. Men are about 40 percent less likely than women to seek counseling for any reason. And the well-documented crisis in male friendship means that many men have no one aside from their spouse or partner they feel they can open up with emotionally. Single men often have no one at all; when they burn out, they may do so alone.

 CD1-23

11 The key problems that distinguish men's burnout share roots in the ethic of stoical duty our society has instilled in boys and men for decades: Go to work, and shut up about it. If you can put food on the table, then you're a good father.

12 The breadwinner ethos is a faulty masculinization of a noble ideal — that even those who do not work still deserve to eat — shared by men and women alike. It's a source of meaning for countless people who labor in difficult conditions so that their children won't have to. It is also hard to live up to. This lingering ideal has been devastating for many blue-collar men, who pinned their self-worth to the notion that they were providers even as their job prospects diminished. Middle-aged and younger men may think this ethos is a relic of their fathers' or grandfathers' era, when fewer women worked full-time. I certainly thought I was past it.

13 But as a society, we are not. The Pew Research Center reported in 2017 that 71 percent of Americans thought "being able to support a family" was important to a man being a good husband, compared with 32 percent who said it was important to a woman being a good wife. Younger respondents were only slightly less committed than average to this ideal of manhood; 64 percent of adults age 18 to 29 said breadwinning was important to being a good husband, while 34 percent said it was important for being a good wife.

⊙ CD1-24

14 My burnout ebbed after we moved to Texas. As a freelance writer and part-time college instructor, I now earn a fraction of what my wife does. I know that isn't my fault; the differential is due to the declining labor conditions of journalism and academia. I care about my work, but it no longer means everything to me. We don't have kids, but at home, I know I'm doing my part.

15 Ultimately, to end our burnout culture, we will need not just better working conditions
75 but new ideals about work's role in human flourishing. That will entail committing to ideals of manhood that rely less on economic productivity and more on virtues like loyalty, solidarity and courage — including the courage to quit a job, raise a child or both.

1,062 words

By Jonathan Malesic, Jan. 4, 2022, The New York Times

Notes

ℓ.1 tenured「終身在職権のある」:
tenure（テニュア制度）はアメリカ、カナダなど北米の大学で採用されている終身在職制度。一定期間の任期で採用された後、任期中の業績や教員の能力に基づいて審査を通過した者に終身在職権が与えられる。tenured professorとはこの権利を付与された教授をさす。本来の目的は教員の学問の自由を守ることにあったが、近年は不定期雇用ではない経済的な安定に重きが置かれるようになった。

ℓ.19 second shift「セカンド・シフト（第2の仕事）」:
共働き女性が日中の仕事から帰宅した後に行う「第2の仕事」、つまり家庭内労働が待ち受けていることをさす。この言葉は、アメリカの社会学者アリー・ホックシールドらが1989年に出版した *The Second Shift: Working Parents and the Revolution at Home* に由来する。

ℓ.32 breadwinner ethos「ブレッドウィナー理論」:
breadwinnerは「稼ぎ頭」という意味で「男性が家庭の大黒柱であるべき」という精神論のことをいう。

ℓ.63 The Pew Research Center「ピュー・リサーチ・センター」:
アメリカ・ワシントンD.C.に本部を置く調査機関。米国の世論調査をはじめ、数多くのテーマについて幅広く調査を行っている。

True or **F**alse | 英文を読んで、本文と合致する場合は T を、合致しない場合は F を記入しましょう。

1. Signs of the writer's burnout appeared in the forms of poor motivation and uncontrollable anger, both of which continued until he quit his job. [   ]

2. Working men and women tend to undergo burnout in a similar way. [   ]

3. One of the reasons why men burn out is that they often have few people to talk to about their problems. [   ]

4. The report by The Pew Research Center showed a big difference between what older and younger generations believed necessary to be a good husband or wife. [   ]

5. In order to end burnout, society must redirect the ideals of manhood, including ones that rely on economic productivity. [   ]

Question & **A**nswer | 次の質問に英文で答えましょう。

1. Why is women's burnout more likely to gain public attention than men's?

_____

2. According to Belgian researchers, how did fathers react to burnout?

_____

3. What does the writer believe is the cause of his current situation where he earns less than his wife?

_____

Correction & **L**istening | 以下は 5 箇所の文法上の誤りを含んだ記事の要約文です。誤りを正しく直しましょう。その後、正しい音声を聞いて答えを確認しましょう。

◉ CD1-25

Traditional, men were the family breadwinners. Despite recent improvements in gender roles, society still has these expectations to some extent. In additionally, society tends to focus on women's burnout and pays small attention to men's burnout. Men who work too hardly may suffer from burnout as well as women. To address this problem, we will need not only better working conditions but also new ideals about the role of work in human happiness. These may include ideals of masculine that rely more on virtues such as loyalty, solidarity, and courage instead of economic productivity.

Reflecting on the Whole Article

本章の記事は著者の一人称で綴られ、個人的な見解を表したオピニオン記事である。「男性側から見た仕事における燃え尽き現象」という具体的なエピソードで読者の関心をつかんだ後、社会全体におけるジェンダーの役割という大きなテーマへと発展させて問題提起をしている。

 以下は記事全体の流れと、キーとなる英文です。ペアまたはグループを作り、これらの英文を読んで感じたことをシェアしましょう。その後、各メンバーで分担して次の質問について考え、答えを発表し合いましょう。

Paragraphs 1 — 3

著者自身の「燃え尽き」体験と退職後の想い

Despite my relief, I felt like a failure not only as an academic, but also as a man.

Q Why do you think he felt like a failure as a man?

Paragraphs 4 — 10

男女間での燃え尽きの差、男性の症状にも注目すべき理由

If we want to end burnout, we have to address the problem for men as well as women.

Q Considering that women's risk of burnout is so much greater, why do we need to pay attention to men's burnout?

Paragraphs 11 — 13

男性の燃え尽きを見えにくくする「男の美学」は今も残る

I certainly thought I was past it[the breadwinner ethos]. But as a society, we are not.

Q Give one example of what society has not yet overcome in terms of manhood.

Paragraphs 14 — 15

燃え尽き後の著者が辿り着いた結論

Ultimately, to end our burnout culture, we will need not just better working conditions but new ideals about work's role in human flourishing.

Q What solutions does the writer suggest about men's burnout?

Discussing the Issues

現代社会には男女ともに燃え尽き症候群になるきっかけが多くあるといえる。以下は、本章の記事に寄せられたコメントである。

 osting Your Comment

次のコメントを参考に、あなた自身の意見を書いてみましょう。

Jonny R, *11 hours ago*
I am a full-time worker with a job in management. I enjoy my work but ultimately we work to live, not live to work. It's important to have a good work-life balance.

Mami, *6 hours ago*
My friend's wife keeps complaining that her husband's salary is too low, but he is happy with his work. What should l say to his wife?

Jessie, *1 hour ago*
Men and women should share the burden equally. Scandinavian countries are showing the way forward, and both men and women are less stressed than in many other countries.

You, *now*

Window to Further Research

どうすれば燃え尽きずに仕事と向き合えるか、それは現代人の大きな課題であると言っても過言ではない。燃え尽きないためにも、状況を客観的に判断し、プライオリティは何かを見極め、適切な人間関係を構築することが重要である。燃え尽きや働き方について考えるには以下の本がおすすめである。

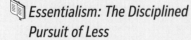 *Essentialism: The Disciplined Pursuit of Less*
by Greg McKeown, Crown Publishing Group, 2014
エッセンシャル思考は本当に重要なことを見極め、確実に実行するためのシステム的方法論である。99%の無駄を捨て1%に集中する方法を提唱する。

 Burnout: The Secret to Unlocking the Stress Cycle
by Emily Nagoski & Amelia Nagoski, Ballantine Books, 2019
多くの女性は、現代社会で期待される女性像と現実とのギャップを埋めようとして燃え尽き症候群となる場合が多い。本書は、社会的圧力を無視するのではなく、思いやりや楽観性から燃え尽きを説明し、具体的な対処方法を提示する。

Bringing Middle Eastern Beer to New York

The Washington Post

Imagine you emigrated to another country and started a business related to Japanese traditional culture. What business would you start and what challenges would you face?

Vocabulary **S**orting | 次の語句をカテゴリーに分類しましょう。未知語はペアで意味を確認しましょう。

farm	manufacturing	zest	bake
brewery	eatery	release	crisp
tart	sour	packaging	roll out
consumer	distribution	taproom	brew

Taste	Place	Production process	Sales
•	•	•	•
•	•	•	•
•	•	•	•
•	•	•	•

Words in **C**ontext | 日本語のヒントを参考に、上の語句から適切な表現を選び、必要な場合は文に合うように形を変えて空欄に記入しましょう。　◉ CD1-26

Beer has ancient roots. Traditionally, brewing was small-scale, but today the
1. _____ process is streamlined. First, a 2. _____ will
　　　　　　製造　　　　　　　　　　　　　　　　　　　　　　　　　　　　　醸造所
3. _____ the beer. After brewing and 4. _____, the beer is
　　　醸造する　　　　　　　　　　　　　　　4.　　　　　　　　　　　　　　梱包
5. _____ to a few bars, where the 6. _____ tries it. If it proves
　　　　発売される　　　　　　　　　　　　　　　　　　　消費者
popular, the manufacturer will then 7. _____ it more widely.
　　　　　　　　　　　　　　　　　　　　　　流通させる

Reading the Article

This one-woman brewery brings Middle Eastern flavor back to craft beer

1 For most of her life, Zahra Tabatabai heard only whispers about her grandfather's beer. Gholam-Reza Fakhrabadi died when Tabatabai was 3 or 4 years old, and her mother and aunts kept his memory alive by mentioning the sumac "Baba Joon" used in his recipes, and her widowed grandmother would recall the lime and orange blossom he picked from
5 his own garden "back home" in Iran. But for Tabatabai, "Baba Joon's ab jo" (Persian for beer), was always a ghost.

2 Growing up in her family's kitchens in and around Atlanta, Tabatabai learned to flavor dishes with traditional Iranian ingredients; barberries for rice, dried black limes and pomegranate molasses for stews. But Baba Joon's ab jo — and simply the idea of Iranian
10 beer — was a more elusive recipe.

3 The 1979 Islamic revolution led to the prohibition of the production, sale and consumption of alcohol. Tabatabai's family arrived in the United States one year earlier, but it wasn't until 2020 that an offhand comment from her grandmother inspired her to brew her birthright into reality. "She said she missed the taste of my grandfather's beer,"
15 Tabatabai said. "I thought I was a pretty good chef; brewing can't be that hard."

⊙ CD1-28

4 Turns out, it was. Tabatabai, 40, who at the time was working as a freelance journalist, had to learn how to brew beer in her Brooklyn apartment. She had to teach herself how to build a business from the ground up through scaling her recipes, manufacturing, packaging and distribution.

20 **5** In October 2021, after months of trial and error at her tiny gas stovetop, stowing and shipping bottles back to Atlanta to get feedback from her family, and some moral support from the local brewing community, Tabatabai decided to open her own brewing company, Back Home Beer — in the middle of a pandemic.

6 Fifteen months later, Tabatabai's nanobrewery is an unlikely success story. According to
25 a recent audit by the Brewers Association, fewer than 24 percent of U.S. craft breweries are woman-owned, and only 2 percent are owned by a person of Asian ethnicity. Tabatabai is one of even fewer brewers making beer influenced by a part of the world that is not closely associated with the industry.

7 She believes that last differentiator, her Middle Eastern spin on familiar beer styles, will
30 be the secret to her success in a saturated marketplace — and at the same time, help her empower immigrants and women in a White-male-dominated beer world.

8 "It was really important for me to share our culture and bring something new to beer," Tabatabai said. "I wanted to bring a new flavor and twist with ingredients that are popular flavor profiles in our cuisine. And I want to educate people about beer in that region."

⊙ CD1-29

35 **9** American-made beer is rooted firmly in European traditions. Even mass-produced American pale lagers, such as Budweiser or Coors Light, are just lighter versions of their Czech and German ancestors.

10 The history of beer goes back much further, to a different part of the globe. The fermenting of ale-style beer using barley started about 5,000 years ago in Mesopotamia,
40 present-day Iraq and parts of Syria and Turkey. And most of the ancient brew masters were

women. "They were responsible for grinding grain for bread and beer; they often baked and brewed in the same spaces," said Theresa McCulla, curator of brewing history at the Smithsonian's National Museum of American History. "The oldest known written recipe for beer is 'The Hymn to Ninkasi' (1800 B.C.), a song of praise and thanks to a brewing
45   woman goddess."

11 While brewing in Europe developed independently, beermaking in the Middle East continued to evolve using the same universal combination of water, grain and yeast. Brewers would add flavors based on the ingredients around them. When Tabatabai's grandfather was brewing in mid-20th-century Iran, this would have included Persian blue
50   salt, barberries, sour cherries, sumac and black limes.

CD1-30

12 These are among the tastes that Tabatabai gathered from her grandmother's, mother's and aunts' memories. Next, she bought a home-brewing kit, consulted staff at local home-brew shop Bitter & Esters, and started bingeing brewing videos and tutorials on YouTube.

13 At the same time, she shared one of her creations, a barberry sour, with a local brewer
55   who was excited to work with her to produce and release it at his Brooklyn brewery. When the pandemic hit, the brewer moved out before the collaboration could become a reality. But the experience gave Tabatabai the extra validation she felt she needed, and in 2021, she contracted space at Staten Island's Flagship Brewing Company and started rolling out kegs and cans for local consumers on her own.

60 **14** Back Home Beer was born with the release of two beers. The Persian Lager is crafted to channel her grandfather's brews: It's a crisp, classic-style lager with a pinch of Persian blue salt sourced from Iran. The Sumac Gose is perhaps Tabatabai's most personal, a slightly tart but not face-twisting sour that pours ruby pink and bursts with the zest of cured sumac sourced from a farm in Turkey and salt and sour cherries from Iran, all ingredients
65   she knows her grandfather used.

15 The response to her releases has been overwhelming, Tabatabai said. In just over a year, Back Home has expanded availability to more than 200 bars and eateries in all five boroughs of New York and into Washington. Now she is focused on finding investors to build her own brewing space that would enable her to scale up production and expand
70   distribution, and a taproom.

16 "I'd like to get the beer to the Southeast, where my family is," she said. "And I'd love a space, ideally in Brooklyn, where there would be Persian street food. It'd be a place for people who might feel out of place at another brewery. That's the dream."

17 Back Home Beer is buttressed by a widespread enthusiasm that's not focused solely on the beer, but also inspired by Tabatabai's message of representation of gender, Middle Eastern roots and the immigrant voice in craft beer. And that message is resonating far beyond her distribution radius.

1,007 words

By Tony Rehagen, Feb. 10, 2023, *The Washington Post*

Notes

ℓ. 3 sumac「スマック」:
ウルシ科の植物で、中東や地中海沿岸地域でスパイスとして使われる。

ℓ. 9 pomegranate molasses「ザクロ糖蜜」:
ザクロの実から抽出されるシロップで、中東料理を代表する食材のひとつ。

ℓ.11 The 1979 Islamic revolution「イラン革命」:
1979年、シーア派宗教指導者ホメイニ率いるイスラム原理主義勢力が、欧米寄りのパフレヴィー朝を倒し、現在のイラン・イスラム共和国 (Islamic Republic of Iran) を樹立した変革をさす。飲酒を含む食生活や文化など、それまでは許容された西欧的な風習は禁止され、女性に外出時のヒジャブ着用を義務付けるなど、厳格なイスラム原理主義に基づく政治体制が敷かれた。

ℓ.24 nanobrewery「ナノブルワリー」:
クラフトビールの多くは小規模の醸造所で生産されるが、当初はmicrobreweryと呼ばれ、年間生産量が15,000バレル (約1,750kℓ) 以下、且つその75%が製造場以外で消費されている醸造所すべてをさしていた。技術の進歩や市場の細分化によりもっと規模の小さい醸造所が出現するようになり、これらをnanobreweryと呼ぶようになった。

ℓ.25 Brewers Association (BA)「醸造家協会」:
5,000以上の醸造者や流通業者、クラフトビールの小売業者などから成るアメリカの業界団体。2005年設立。この団体ではクラフトビール (ここでの英語は craft brewer) の定義を「小規模で、独立していて、伝統がある」としていて、この定義が世界的にも一般的となっている。

ℓ.36 American pale lagers「アメリカンペールラガー」:
ビールはモルト (麦芽) を発酵させてつくるが、高温で酵母を浮き上がらせてつくるものを「エール」、低温で酵母を沈めてつくるものを「ラガー」と呼ぶ。アメリカンペールラガーは後者の一つで、軽めで炭酸が強いのが特徴。日本の主要ビールもほとんどがラガーに大別されるが、アメリカンペールラガーよりも苦味とコクがあるのが特徴。

ℓ.44 The Hymn to Ninkasi「ニンカシ讃歌」:
ニンカシは古代メソポタミアにおけるビール醸造を司る女神で、「ニンカシ讃歌」はこの女神を讃える歌であると同時に、古代醸造法のレシピでもある。レシピを歌にしたのは口頭伝承しやすいためといわれる。

英文を読んで、本文と合致する場合はTを、合致しない場合はFを記入しましょう。

1. Tabatabai seldom learned traditional Iranian dishes from her family. [ ]

2. The nanobrewery of Persian beer became a big success in just over a year. [ ]

3. Twenty-four percent of craft breweries in the U.S. are run by people of Asian ethnicity. [ ]

4. Women played a central role in brewing ale-style beer in Mesopotamia. [ ]

5. The collaboration with a local brewer to release barberry sour at his brewery was a big success. [ ]

Question & Answer

次の質問に英文で答えましょう。

1. What inspired Tabatabai to start brewing her grandfather's beer?

_____

2. How did beermaking in the Middle East develop?

_____

3. What does Tabatabai dream to do in Brooklyn?

_____

Correction & Listening

以下は5箇所の文法上の誤りを含んだ記事の要約文です。誤りを正しく直しましょう。その後、正しい音声を聞いて答えを確認しましょう。

CD1-31

　　Zahra Tabatabai is an enthusiastic brewer whose owns a company in New York called Back Home Beer. Although the beer industry is a saturated market, Tabatabai came up with the idea of introduce a beer with a Middle Eastern spin that had been her grandfather's recipe. After some trials and error and with the support of her family and the local community, she released two beers. The new flavors were a big success. Now she is realizing her dream of release beers in her family's hometown in the Southeast and opening a place on Brooklyn for people who may feel out of place at other breweries.

Reflecting on the Whole Article

タバタバイ氏のサクセスストーリーの背景には彼女が自身のルーツを大事にする想いがあり、それを記事の随所から感じ取ることができる。本記事は、時系列を追って情報を整理しやすい構成となっており、その中でタバタバイ氏自身の言葉が記事全体に抑揚をつけている。

 以下は記事全体の流れと、キーとなる英文です。ペアまたはグループを作り、これらの英文を読んで感じたことをシェアしましょう。その後、各メンバーで分担して次の質問について考え、答えを発表し合いましょう。

Paragraphs 1 – 3

イランビール醸造の契機 —— 祖父の味を復活させたい

For most of her life, Zahra Tabatabai heard only whispers about her grandfather's beer.

Q Why do you think Tabatabai heard only "whispers" about the beer?

Paragraphs 4 – 8

Back Home Beer の立ち上げとタバタバイ氏の想い、ビール業界の実情

"It was really important for me to share our culture and bring something new to beer" (Zahra Tabatabai)

Q What does she mean by this?

Paragraphs 9 – 11

古代に遡るビールの歴史 —— 中東独自のフレーバー

The history of beer goes back much further, to a different part of the globe.

Q When did ale-style beer brewing begin, and what kind of ingredients were added by the 20th century?

Paragraphs 12 – 17

タバタバイ氏の奮闘、念願の発売と大きな反響、彼女の今後の展望

"And I'd love a space, ... It'd be a place for people who might feel out of place at another brewery. That's the dream." (Zahra Tabatabai)

Q What kind of people do you think she may be referring to?

Discussing the Issues

小さなビジネスが大きく成長するための秘策は何であろうか。以下は、本章の記事に寄せられたコメントである。

Posting Your **C**omment | 次のコメントを参考に、あなた自身の意見を書いてみましょう。

Steve, *5 hours ago*
The rarity of the beer style has contributed to the big hit, of course, but her spirit of never giving up and dreaming big must have been key to the success of her business.

Matilda, *4 hours ago*
I think it took a lot of courage for Tabatabai to start a business in a completely different industry. Also, her ability to involve others, such as her family and the community, is inspiring.

Health nut, *3 hours ago*
I heard that the number of startup companies in Japan is much smaller than in the U.S. I wonder what the reasons are. A comparative lack of financial support may be one reason.

You, *now*
_____
_____
_____

Window to Further Research

多様性の時代と言われる現代で、自分の道を見つけて前向きに生きていく力はいったいどこからくるのだろうか。以下は自身のアイデンティティを武器に成功を収めた人の物語である。どのような共通要素があるだろうか。

Finding Me: A Memoir
by Viola Davis, HarperCollins Publishers, 2022

1960年代のアメリカで、アフリカ系アメリカ人に対する差別と貧困に苦しむ少女が、トラウマを克服しながら役者という天職によって救われる自伝。邦題『天職が魂の救済になる日まで』。

『クラフトビール革命 地域を変えた　アメリカの小さな地ビール起業』
スティーブ・ヒンディ著、和田侑子（訳）、DU BOOKS、2015年

元ジャーナリストでもあり、ブルックリンをクラフトビールの一大メッカにしたNYブルックリン・ブルワリー創業者による、起業から事業を成功させるまでのルポ。

The New York Times

Basic Information

創立　1851年
創業者　ヘンリー・ジャーヴィス・レイモンド、
　　　　ジョージ・ジョーンズ
形態　日刊紙
本社　アメリカ合衆国ニューヨーク州
スローガン
　　印刷に値するニュースはすべて掲載する
　　(All The News That's Fit To Print)

　ワシントン・ポストと並ぶ、アメリカを代表する高級紙。タイムズ（The Times）と呼ばれることも多く、ニューヨークの名所タイムズ・スクエアは1904年にタイムズ本社が同地に移転してきたことにちなむ（現在の本社は少し西のニューヨーク・タイムズ・ビルディング）。1851年に「ニューヨーク・デイリー・タイムズ」として発刊。一時破産の危機に陥るも、1896年に同社を買収したアドルフ・オックスが立て直しに成功し（上記のスローガンもこのときに誕生した）、オックス死後は娘婿アーサー・ヘイズ・サルツバーガーが引き継ぎ、以後もサルツバーガー家が経営の実権を握っている。

　政治記事と社会記事におけるリベラルな論調が特徴で、大統領選挙などでもそのスタンスを明確に表明する。近年では特に調査報道に力を入れ、そこから後述するワインスタインの報道なども生まれた。またデジタル移行にも積極的で、2022年にはデジタルの有料読者数が100万人を突破した。

#MeToo運動に火をつけた
映画界の大物によるセクハラ暴露

　タイムズの調査報道記者で、それまで女性問題を中心に追ってきたジョディ・カンターと、2016年にドナルド・トランプのセクハラ報道をスクープした同僚のミーガン・トゥーイーは、ハリウッドに君臨する大物プロデューサー、ハーヴェイ・ワインスタインが長年にわたって女優やスタッフに性的行為を強要していた事実をオフレコでつかむ。しかし、被害者の多くは示談金と引き換えに秘密保持契約を結ばせられたり、脅迫などを恐れて公（オンレコ）にしようとはしなかった。さらに、調査を嗅ぎつけたワインスタイン側も取材を執拗に妨害する。しかし、二人の粘り強い取材に、女優アシュレイ・ジャッドを筆頭に声が上がり始め、裏取りや物的証拠を押さえたのち2017年10月に告発記事を公開。この記事は大きな反響を呼び、その後映画界のみならず、いろいろな分野でのセクハラの告発が続き、このうねりは#MeToo運動へと発展する。二人の記者はこれでピュリツァー賞を受賞。その後著作『その名を暴け』にまとめられ、2022年に『シー・セッド その名を暴け（原題：She Said）』として映画化された。映画ではカンターをゾーイ・カザン、トゥーイーをキャリー・マリガンが演じ、ジャッドも本人役で登場する。

Stories
of The World We Live In

III

DIVERSIFY

Chapter 6

The Runner Who Took a Stand

The Guardian

Have you ever made a stand? Perhaps you have disagreed strongly with your classmates, or even taken part in a demonstration. If you haven't, then why haven't you?

Vocabulary Sorting

次の語句をカテゴリーに分類しましょう。未知語はペアで意味を確認しましょう。

civil rights march	win bronze	get chills	pivotal moment
in the eye of the storm	under the radar	boycott	assassination
Olympic podium	sharecropper	boo	regarded as traitors
hold 11 records concurrently	followed suit	shun	sporting potential

African American experience	Sport	Negative action / emotion	Metaphor
•	•	•	•
•	•	•	•
•	•	•	•
•	•	•	•

Words in Context

日本語のヒントを参考に、上の語句から適切な表現を選び、必要な場合は文に合うように形を変えて空欄に記入しましょう。　　　　◉ CD2-02

Martin Luther King was a key figure in the **1.** _____
（公民権デモ行進）
of the 1960s. A **2.** _____ occurred when a black woman
（とても重要な瞬間）
named Rosa Parks refused to give up her seat for a white woman, and many others soon
3. _____. Black people were outraged and began a boycott of the buses,
（後に続いた）
which they **4.** _____ in large numbers. As a prominent figure in the civil
（避けた）
rights movement, King was always **5.** _____. Some people
（渦中に）
still **6.** _____ when they remember King's tragic **7.** _____.
（ぞっとする）　　　　　　　　　　　　　　　　　　　　　　　　　　　　　　　　　　　　（暗殺）

Reading the Article

 CD2-03

'People shunned me like hot lava': the runner who raised his fist and risked his life

1 Tommie Smith still gets chills when he hears the opening bars of The Star Spangled Banner. It takes him right back to that night in October 1968 when he stood on the Olympic podium in Mexico City, wearing his gold medal, and made the raised-fist salute that has defined his life. In the months leading up to the Olympics, he had been receiving death
5 threats. Two weeks before, Mexican police had fired into a crowd of student protesters, killing as many as 300 people. Martin Luther King had been assassinated just six months earlier. So there was a real possibility that somebody in the stadium might try to shoot him or his team-mate John Carlos, who was making the salute beside him after winning bronze.

10 **2** Sports and politics are once more in the eye of the storm, but Smith's life shows how

inseparable the two have always been, especially for a Black man who grew up in the U.S. after the second world war. For Smith, the two were fused together permanently one weekend in March 1965. At an athletics meet on a Saturday, Smith broke his first world records — for the 200m and 220 yards (simultaneously as the track had two finish lines).

15 He then went to join, part-way along, his first civil rights march, a 45-mile walk from San Jose to San Francisco calling for equal educational opportunities. It was a pivotal moment for him. "We were one of the first student marches for a good cause in the history of the United States," he says. "We were booed by the cars passing. Things were thrown at us." They arrived in San Francisco, Smith having walked 30 miles, on Sunday evening.

CD2-04

20 **3** Smith credits his hard childhood for his athletic ability. In effect, his training began as soon as he could walk, and work. He was the seventh of 14 siblings, two of whom died, in a poor family in rural Texas. As with most Black families in the area, they were sharecroppers — working land owned by white people, who took most of the profits. In the Jim Crow south, Smith barely ever saw any white people, he says, or any other people

25 at all; the nearest neighbours were several miles away. The whole family worked in the cotton fields and lived in a leaky wooden house.

4 At high school, Smith's sporting potential shone through — that earned him a scholarship to San Jose State University, where he studied sociology. Smith was learning African American history, even as the civil rights movement was writing a new chapter

30 of it. This was the era of the March on Washington; Martin Luther King's Birmingham protests; the Alabama church bombings, in which four young Black girls were killed by the Ku Klux Klan; the assassination of Malcolm X. African Americans were standing up, and being beaten down. Smith felt he needed to act. "I read sociology, but I didn't *do* sociology," he says. "I realised that reading was not good enough. You got to lay that book

35 down and apply to the system what you learned in the book that the system wrote. And a lot of time it wasn't Black folks that wrote it; it was other cultures that wrote it."

5 At the same time, Smith was going from strength to strength on the track: the Usain Bolt of his day. Tall, rangy and well trained, he dominated men's sprinting. In 1968, he held 11 world records concurrently, across 200m and 400m. There was little question he would

40 be on the U.S. Olympics team for Mexico 1968.

CD2-05

6 The year before, African American athletes had discussed boycotting the Olympics. In October 1967, the activist and academic Harry Edwards formed what became the Olympic

Project for Human Rights (OPHR), along with Smith, Carlos and the 400m runner Lee Evans (all four were at San Jose State). The goal was human rights, Smith stresses, not Black power. The OPHR had a set of demands: that apartheid South Africa and Rhodesia be excluded; that Muhammad Ali's world heavyweight boxing title, removed as punishment for his stance against the Vietnam war, be reinstated; and that more African American coaches be hired.

7 On the podium, Smith and Carlos' clothes carried important symbolism. They only had one pair of gloves between them; Smith and Carlos' right hand signified "the power within Black America," he told reporters at the time, while Carlos's left hand stood for "Black unity." The black scarf around Smith's neck stood for Black pride. They wore black socks without shoes to symbolise "Black poverty in racist America." Carlos's bead necklace was for the lynchings of Black Americans. In addition, Smith, Carlos and the silver medallist, the Australian Peter Norman, all wore OPHR badges.

8 Most of (white) America regarded them as traitors. "When I came back to California, people shunned me like I was hot lava," Smith says. "I had a young son and a wife and I had to work, but the only jobs I could find were, like, washing cars. Had I been a white guy who held 11 world records, I believe no matter what I would have done in Mexico City or in the Olympic Games, I would have had some backing."

(O) CD2-06

9 During the 70s, Smith went under the radar. He finished his final year of college, then played football for the Cincinnati Bengals for a couple of seasons, before moving into teaching and athletics coaching, first at Oberlin College, near Cleveland, then in Santa Monica. Over the decades, his moral stand came to be recognised and celebrated. The image of Smith and Carlos on the podium is now part of civil rights history — reproduced on T-shirts and posters, recreated in music videos, commemorated in statues and murals, chronicled in documentaries.

10 In 2016, by way of a belated apology, they were invited to be Olympic ambassadors for the U.S. team in Rio. After the games, President Obama honoured them at the White House. "Their powerful silent protest in the 1968 Games was controversial, but it woke folks up and created greater opportunity for those that followed," he said.

11 Perhaps Smith's greatest vindication is that he set a powerful example for other sportspeople to use their platforms. The obvious parallel is Colin Kaepernick, whose

decision to kneel during the national anthem in 2016 to highlight police racism caused
75 similar controversy, and fed into the momentous Black Lives Matter movement. Other
leading sportspeople have followed suit: Serena Williams, Lewis Hamilton, LeBron James
and Naomi Osaka, not to mention England's national football team.

12 "Sports and politics, in my terminology of moving forward and the truth, have always
been a part of each other," Smith continues. "I didn't wear red, white and blue because
80 they're my favourite colours. You don't sing the national anthem because it has a cool beat."

1,133 words

By Steve Rose, Oct. 14, 2021, *The Guardian*

Notes

ℓ.1　The Star Spangled Banner「星条旗(アメリカ国歌)」:
言わずとしれたアメリカ国歌で、スポーツの国際大会など大きなイベントでよく斉唱されるが、作詞をした詩人・弁護士のフランシス・スコット・キーは奴隷制度を奨励したことでも知られ、歌詞の中にも奴隷を侮蔑したような表現があるとして、近年(特にBLM運動後)はこれを国歌とするのを問題視する動きが出ている。

ℓ.24　Jim Crow (laws)「ジム・クロウ法」:
アメリカ南部における黒人差別の法体系。ジム・クロウとは1828年に上演され流行したミュージカルの黒人登場人物の名が由来で、その後黒人の蔑称となった。この法により公共施設や教育機関での人種隔離・投票権の実質的な剥奪といった黒人の不当な扱いが合法とされてきた。この法の撤廃は1960年代の公民権運動時代まで待たねばならなかった。

ℓ.30　the March on Washington「ワシントン大行進」:
公民権運動が盛り上がりを見せる中、1963年8月28日にアメリカ・ワシントンD.C.で25万人以上の平和的デモ隊が人種差別撤廃を求めて大行進を行った。キング牧師が「I Have a Dream」の演説を行ったことでも有名。

ℓ.30　Martin Luther King's Birmingham protests「バーミングハム運動におけるキング牧師の抗議」:
キング牧師と南部キリスト教指導者会議による公民権運動の一つで、アフリカ系アメリカ人に対する不平等な法律を変える圧力となった。

ℓ.32　Ku Klux Klan「クー・クラックス・クラン」:
プロテスタントのアングロサクソン系白人を神に選ばれし民とする選民思想を持ち、主に黒人、アジア、ヒスパニック系の人種に対し強い差別意識を持つ白人至上主義団体。

ℓ.42　the Olympic Project for Human Rights (OPHR)「人権を求めるオリンピック・プロジェクト」:
社会学者ハリー・エドワーズのほか、トミー・スミスやジョン・カルロスなどの有名選手によって設立されたスポーツにおける人種差別に抗議する組織。

ℓ.55　Peter Norman「ピーター・ノーマン」:
1968年メキシコオリンピック男子200mの銀メダリスト。男子短距離走でのメダル獲得は母国のオーストラリアにとって史上初の快挙だった。しかし、同氏の表彰式での行動は白豪主義思想が色濃く残る母国で大きく非難され、その後の選手生命は事実上絶たれることとなる。

True or **F**alse | 英文を読んで、本文と合致する場合は T を、合致しない場合は F を記入しましょう。

1. The Mexican police once fired into the crowd at an athletics event that Smith attended.
[   ]

2. Smith became athletic by regularly walking 30 miles an evening. [   ]

3. Smith lived in Jim Crow's household far from any neighbors. [   ]

4. Smith founded the Olympic Project for Human Rights after the Mexico Olympics.
[   ]

5. Movements such as Black Lives Matter were indirectly influenced by Tommie Smith.
[   ]

 Question & **A**nswer | 次の質問に英文で答えましょう。

1. How did Smith's family make a living in Texas?

_____

2. According to Smith, how might responses to what he did at the Olympics have been different if he were a white athlete?

_____

3. What influence has Smith's action had on today's leading sportspeople?

_____

Correction & **L**istening | 以下は5箇所の文法上の誤りを含んだ記事の要約文です。誤りを正しく直しましょう。その後、正しい音声を聞いて答えを確認しましょう。

⊙ CD2-07

Tommie Smith took a stand for racism when he made a raised-fist salute on the winners' podium in Mexico City. He was very bravery to do this in a dangerous political climate. Smith had grown up in poverty, but he managed to win a scholarship to a university. After great succeed at the 1968 Olympics, people shunned him because to his political stance. He then played football and went into academia. His image in the podium is now a part of civil rights history and he is a respected role model.

Reflecting on the Whole Article

本章の記事ではトミー・スミス氏の個人的体験が当時の歴史的背景の中で語られることで、問題の中身をより鮮明に浮かび上がらせる効果を生んでいる。スミス氏の体験や発言の背景にどんな問題や意図があったのかを考えながら読むと、より理解を深めることができる。

 以下は記事全体の流れと、キーとなる英文です。ペアまたはグループを作り、これらの英文を読んで感じたことをシェアしましょう。その後、各メンバーで分担して次の質問について考え、答えを発表し合いましょう。

Paragraphs **1 − 2**

スミス氏がオリンピック表彰台に立った夜の回想、スポーツと政治の問題

Tommie Smith still gets chills when he hears the opening bars of The Star Spangled Banner.

Q Why does the sound of The Star Spangled Banner still give Tommie Smith chills?

Paragraphs **3 − 5**

スミス氏の半生——幼少時代、アスリートの才能開花、公民権運動の時代に大学で学んだこと

"I read sociology, but I didn't do *sociology"* (Tommie Smith)

Q What does Smith mean by this?

Paragraphs **6 − 8**

OPHRの設立、命をかけたオリンピックでの抗議活動

On the podium, Smith and Carlos' clothes carried important symbolism.

Q Smith and Carlos place great importance on symbolism. Explain why Smith felt the need to display symbolism.

Paragraphs **9 − 12**

時を経て認められたスミス氏の功績、後世のアスリート達への影響

"Their powerful silent protest in the 1968 Games was controversial, but it woke folks up and created greater opportunity for those that followed" (President Obama)

Q What opportunities do you think President Obama was referring to?

Discussing the Issues

近年、スポーツ界における人種差別への闘いについての議論が再燃している。以下は本章の記事に寄せられたコメントである。

Posting Your **C**omment | 次のコメントを参考に、あなた自身の意見を書いてみましょう。

> **TY,** *9 hours ago*
> As a track athlete who is studying at university, I have great admiration for Tommie Smith. I think students should follow his example and take a stand also. I personally admire Colin Kaepernick protesting by refusing to stand when singing the national anthem before the big game.

> **tonystoke,** *4 hours ago*
> I agree that it is important to take a stand against racism, but I also believe sport should be kept out of politics. I'm not sure if displaying messages of protest in sports matches, like Naomi Osaka does with her tennis wear, is a good thing to do.

> **You,** *now*
> _____
> _____
> _____

Window to Further Research

2020年にアフリカ系アメリカ人の男性ジョージ・フロイドさんが白人警官に拘束され亡くなった事件に象徴されるように、黒人差別の社会的・構造的な問題はいまだに根強く残る。差別の根底にある思想や近年のブラック・ライブズ・マター運動の流れを知るのに、以下の文献がおすすめである。

The Origin of Others
by Toni Morrison, Harvard University Press, 2017

人には帰属意識があり、自分のグループに属さない人を「アウトサイダー」として排斥しがちである。トニ・モリソンは、そのような心理的傾向と歴史的背景、白人崇拝思想といった観点から、なぜアメリカが肌の色に執着するのか、その原因と結果について考察する。

『世界を動かす変革の力 ——ブラック・ライブズ・マター共同代表からのメッセージ』
アリシア・ガーザ著、明石書店、2021年

ブラック・ライブズ・マター運動共同創始者の著書。公民権運動の歴史を礎に、これからは女性や多様な背景を持つ人々の視点を含んだ「分散型リーダーシップ」の力で人種的マイノリティの力を輝かせる時代であると説く。

Chapter 7

Reshaping the Values of Beauty

The Guardian

When you see fashion ads on the internet or in magazines, what do you think of them?
How much do you identify with the featured models?

| 次の語句をカテゴリーに分類しましょう。未知語はペアで意味を確認しましょう。

mascara	transgender	Eurocentric	queer
prejudice	conventional	lip balm	fatphobic
mainstream	eyeshadow	non-binary	blush
normalize	sexist		

Gender identity / Sexual orientation	Cosmetics	Bias	Commonplace
•	•	•	•
•	•	•	•
•	•	•	•
	•	•	

Words in **C**ontext | 日本語のヒントを参考に、上の語句から適切な表現を選び、必要な場合は文に合うように形を変えて空欄に記入しましょう。　　○ CD2-08

The fashion industry has featured models who are almost always slim. This has

1. _____ the idea that slim is the only acceptable body shape, and led some
   標準化した

people to become 2. _____. World-famous models are often Caucasian, showing
                      肥満恐怖症のある

a 3. _____ bias, but diversity is increasing and may one day become
      ヨーロッパ中心主義

4. _____. A recent trend is to feature 5. _____ models.
      主流   トランスジェンダー

In the future, models may give up make-up, such as 6. _____. The idea of artificially
                                                        頬紅

enhancing beauty will seem outdated as we finally come to embrace our natural selves.

COLORS THAT SCREAM

"I'll probably leave your text message on read."

Maybebabie
Decent makeup, ridiculously overpriced.

Reading the Article

 CD2-09

'It's sheer! It's queer!' : redesigning and diversifying beauty ads of the past

1 Long before makeup moguls like Jeffree Star and Kylie Jenner were selling lip kits and mystery boxes on Instagram, there was the old-fashioned way of selling beauty products — in the pages of women's magazines. Thin white women posed alongside phrases like "Lashes" or "Great look, great body, great mascara!" while donning blue eyeshadow and 5 bright bursts of pink blush.

2 These ads are now being reshaped for 2021 with a diverse range of models in the spotlight, from queer to trans and non-binary. Prim-n-Poppin is an online exhibition featuring faux beauty ads shot in an old school style — bright eyeshadow, cheesy smiles and of course, updated phrases that reflect today.

10 **3** The series is co-created by New York photographer Julia Comita and makeup artist

Brenna Drury and aims to challenge outdated beauty standards. It shows how far we've come over the past 50 years, and how far we still need to go.

4 "We asked ourselves: 'What would the future look like today if these advertisements had been the standard of the past?'" asks Drury. "As creatives, we want to challenge the industry to take responsibility for their marketing and diversify their talent pool."

5 The images riff on vintage ads promoting Sally Hansen nail polish, Maybelline eyeshadow, flavored lip balm and frothy face soap alongside racially diverse and LGBTQ models. Each ad is shot in hues of cool pinks and pastel blues, with phrases like: "It's sheer! It's queer!" and "Colors that scream 'I'll probably leave your text message on read.'"

6 "They're supposed to look like vintage ads, we tried to be as authentic as we could with graphic design and photography from the period, which normalizes the talent that's in it," said Comita. "If you're only accustomed to one standard of beauty, that's awful. It had a negative effect on so many people growing up. It shouldn't be like that."

CD2-10

7 One shows trans model Maria Rivera posing with a rainbow palette of eyeshadow, accompanied by a radiating smile. She explains that she always had a dream of working in the beauty industry while growing up in the Philippines. "I have always been a believer of sincere inclusivity regardless of your race, color, gender and body size," said Rivera. "Beauty doesn't come only in one size or color or in one shape of a box, it is universal, and everybody is beautiful in our own way."

8 One of the biggest problems, says Rivera, is tokenism from brands who want to use trans models, for example, only during pride month in June. "To eliminate tokenism in the mainstream, we need to go out and take up our own space," said Rivera. "We need not be afraid or scared to be rejected, rather we need to embrace our differences and accept our uniqueness. Only then will others see the beauty within us."

9 Comita and Drury wanted each model to not only be seen but heard. They've included the voices of each model on the project's website, as the project aims to show the diversity that was missing at the time, and hear what each model has to say about the past, present and potential future.

10 The duo reached out to different modeling agencies that focus on diversity and ones that represent the trans community. "Moving forward I hope more agencies expand their talent pool," she adds.

CD2-11

11 This kind of project calls to mind the story of Tracey "Africa" Norman, a transgender model who worked for Clairol, Avon and Balenciaga in the 1970s — but had to hide it. She only told her story in 2015 about how she made history as the first black trans model, and how dangerous her life was back then.

12 "Now, people have models who look like them, showing possibilities are a lot wider than what they're accustomed to," said Drury. "It's great people are represented more but there's still so far to go."

13 Other models featured in the series include Cory Walker, who says that old school beauty advertising made them "feel invisible in a lot of ways," as well as Kaguya, who wants to see the beauty industry be inclusive of size and age range. "The public in general is still very fatphobic and close-minded," said Kaguya.

14 Cecilio Asuncion, the scouting director of Slay Model Management, says that employment is always an issue in the trans community. "It's important to highlight and underline many definitions of beauty, not just the cis-het, Eurocentric kind that has been served to us for decades if not, centuries," said Asuncion, who represents Rivera.

15 He says projects like Prim-n-Poppin are important as a form of social commentary. "Once people start conversations about beauty diversity, companies and brands take notice," he said, "which will turn into more opportunities."

CD2-12

16 Comita says they hope to expand on the project and hopefully have an exhibition down the line, "that's the dream," she said.

17 The 1970s were used as inspiration, as it was a time which was somewhat relatable, according to the photographer. It wasn't the stiff 1950s, where many ads catered to housewives, or the 1960s, which were still conventional, and had overt racist and sexist overtones.

18 The pictures do have something dreamy or heavenly about them, be it the pastel palette or the pensive gaze of each model. Yet they use the past to show us a potential future of the beauty industry.

19 "For me, this project represents all the young transgender dreams of having freedom to choose," said Rivera. "And to live their lives without any prejudice or need to fit the society's mold and norms."

918 words

By Nadja Sayej, Feb. 3, 2021, The Guardian

Notes

ℓ.30 tokenism「トークニズム（形式主義、体裁主義）」：
人種やジェンダー、環境などの問題に対し表面的には対処しているような態度をとるが、それにより本質的な問題解決を回避しようとする場当たり的な姿勢をさす。この用語は公民権運動が活発化した1960年代に、連邦政府や自治体の差別撤廃政策を批判する際によく使われ、その後一般的になった。日本では多くの企業がSDGsを掲げていながら、一方で環境破壊や労働搾取などに目を瞑っている状況に対し、トークニズムだという批判も一部で起きている。

ℓ.42 Tracey "Africa" Norman「トレイシー・アフリカ・ノーマン」：
1970年代にアメリカで活躍したファッションモデル。自身がトランスジェンダーであることを隠しながらVogue ItaliaやEssenceなどの有名雑誌でモデルとして頭角を表したが、1980年にそれが明るみになり、当時の社会には受け入れられることなく、アメリカでのモデル業を断念せざるを得ない状況となった。その後、再び注目を集めるようになり、トランスジェンダーモデルとしてファッション業界に復帰を果たした。

ℓ.52 fatphobic「肥満恐怖症のある」：
phobiaは「恐怖症」を意味し、fatphobiaは「肥満に対する恐怖心や病的な嫌悪」をさす。fatphobicはその形容詞形。近年は昔からの「スリム＝美」という概念から脱却して、自分に合った体形を美とする考え方＝body positive（ボディポジティブ）がファッション業界で主流になりつつあるが、それでも肥満に対する嫌悪や中傷（これをfat-shamingという）は後を絶たない。

ℓ.53 Slay Model Management「スレイ・モデル・マネージメント」：
2016年に設立された、世界初のトランスジェンダーに特化したモデルエージェンシー。本社はロサンゼルス。2023年にはフィリピンのマニラに支社を作り、アジアでの展開も開始した。

ℓ.55 cis-het「生まれ持った性別と性自認の性別が一致した異性愛者」：
生まれ持った性別と心の性が一致していて、その性別に従って生きる人を意味するcisgender（シスジェンダー）と異性愛者を意味するheterosexual（ヘテロセクシュアル）を組み合わせた語。

True or **F**alse | 英文を読んで、本文と合致する場合は T を、合致しない場合は F を記入しましょう。

1. Prim-n-Poppin publishes beauty ads in print with various models and phrases that reflect today's values. [   ]

2. Julia Comita thinks knowing only one standard of beauty had a bad influence on people as they grew up. [   ]

3. Tracey "Africa" Norman did not talk about her identity as a trans model until 2015. [   ]

4. According to Cecilio Asuncion, the definition of beauty mostly centered on cis-het or European images for quite a long time. [   ]

5. The 1970s inspired this project because the time was more relatable than the conventional and prejudiced images of the 1950s and 1960s. [   ]

 Question & **A**nswer | 次の質問に英文で答えましょう。

1. Why did Comita and Drury challenge the beauty industry?

_____

2. What is problematic when brands use diverse models?

_____

3. Why did Comita and Drury include the voices of each model on the website?

_____

Correction & **L**istening | 以下は 5 箇所の文法上の誤りを含んだ記事の要約文です。誤りを正しく直しましょう。その後、正しい音声を聞いて答えを確認しましょう。

🔘 CD2-13

　　The online exhibition "Prim-n-Poppin" features faux beauty ads in a vintage style with a modern twist, challenging outdated beauty standard. The series showcases diverse models, including queer, trans, and non-binary individuals, promoting beauty products with phrases reflecting today's inclusive. The project aims to encourage the industry to embrace diverse and eliminate tokenism. Each model voice is highlighted on the website to emphasize their unique experiences. By evoking the 1970, the ads present a potential future for the beauty industry that embraces freedom of choice and challenges societal norms.

Reflecting on the Whole Article

長い間画一的であった美の基準が多様化し、型にはまらない個性が輝く機会が増える一方で、いまだ残る美容業界の課題やモデル達が直面する壁がリアルに描かれている。本記事はさまざまな背景を持つモデルや関係者の言葉が多く紹介されている。「挑戦はまだ続く」というクリエイターの言葉も繰り返し伝えられており、彼らの想いの強さと美の定義が今後さらに広がる可能性を示唆している。

 以下は記事全体の流れと、キーとなる英文です。ペアまたはグループを作り、これらの英文を読んで感じたことをシェアしましょう。その後、各メンバーで分担して次の質問について考え、答えを発表し合いましょう。

Paragraphs **1** — **6**

これまでの美容広告に物申す——Prim-n-Poppin の挑戦

It [Prim-n-Poppin] shows how far we've come over the past 50 years, and how far we still need to go.

Q How has Prim-n-Poppin come a long way?

Paragraphs **7** — **10**

広告モデルの美に対する価値観、制作者の願い「モデルの声を届けたい」

... the project aims to show the diversity that was missing at the time, and hear what each model has to say about the past, present and potential future.

Q What is Maria Rivera's vision of a "potential future"?

Paragraphs **11** — **15**

1970年代のトランスジェンダーモデルの例、変わりゆく美の定義に社会は対応できるのか

"It's great people are represented more but there's still so far to go." (Brenna Drury)

Q What problems remain for LGBTQ models in the fashion industry?

Paragraphs **16** — **19**

Prim-n-Poppin の背景にあるもの——過去を通して未来を見る

Yet they [Comita and Drury] use the past to show us a potential future of the beauty industry.

Q Why do you think Comita and Drury use the past to show the potential future?

Discussing the Issues

近年、日本でもさまざまな場面で多様性を受け入れる「インクルーシブ」という理念が注目されている。以下は、本章の記事に寄せられたコメントである。

Posting Your **C**omment | 次のコメントを参考に、あなた自身の意見を書いてみましょう。

Fashion freak, *8 hours ago*
It's nice that people see more models they can relate to, but don't the majority of us tend to admire something that we don't have or that's different from ourselves … especially when it comes to beauty?

Cinnamon, *6 hours ago*
I think it's great that everybody wants to show who they identify as gender-wise by using makeup and colorful clothes. If it becomes widely recognized, it will gradually be accepted as a common value.

Retired teacher, *2 hours ago*
I understand that they value diversity, but then, shouldn't we also accept the beauty standards of the past as well? I think the push towards diversity has gone too far now.

You, *now*
_____
_____
_____

Window to Further Research

近年ファッションや化粧品業界において、多様の美がますます追求されている。その社会的背景となる歴史的な変遷や、業界から実際にどのようにして既成概念を取り払い新しい価値観を生み出したのかを学ぶには以下の本がおすすめである。

Queer x Design: 50 Years of Signs, Symbols, Banners, Logos and Graphic Art of LGBTQ
by Andy Campbell, Black Dog & Leventhal, 2019
アメリカのLGBTQの50年間にわたる歴史とデザイン史についてそれぞれ例を挙げて紹介する編纂書。

A Visible Man: A Memoir
by Edward Enninful, Penguin Press, 2022
雑誌「ヴォーグ」の黒人編集者による回顧録。自身の人生物語と、高齢者や障碍者たちの美の追求を振り返りながら、どのようにしてファッション哲学を変えたかを描いている。

Chapter 8

A Social Media Minefield: Hijab Removal Case in School

The Washington Post

When incidents concerning discrimination or harassment go viral on the internet, how can we determine the facts?

Vocabulary Sorting

次の語句をカテゴリーに分類しましょう。未知語はペアで意味を確認しましょう。

apologize	prosecutor	attorney	condemn
threat	lawsuit	anti-Muslim	abuse
racist	appreciative	respect	gentle
antisemitism	Islamophobia	settlement	

Discrimination	Legal term	Offensive act	Good manner
·	·	·	·
·	·	·	·
·	·	·	·
·	·	·	·

Words in Context

日本語のヒントを参考に、上の語句から適切な表現を選び、必要な場合は文に合うように形を変えて空欄に記入しましょう。   ◎ CD2-14

After the attacks in New York on September 11, 2001, **1.** _____,
<small>イスラム恐怖症</small>
meaning discrimination against Muslims, began to grow in schools. This can take
the form of verbal **2.** _____, or even **3.** _____, against Muslim students.
<small>罵り</small> <small>脅迫</small>
4. _____, or discrimination against Jewish people, also occurs
<small>反ユダヤ主義</small>
sometimes. The situation grows so serious that in some cases **5.** _____ result. We
<small>訴訟</small>
need to treat each other with greater **6.** _____ and be **7.** _____ of
<small>尊敬の念</small> <small>感謝して</small>
the benefits that diversity can bring.

Reading the Article

 CD2-15

She pushed back her student's hijab. Was it a mistake or an act of hate?

1 MAPLEWOOD, N.J. — Tamar Herman knew that a Muslim girl in her second-grade class always wore a hijab. But one day, Herman thought she saw a hoodie covering it. She asked the girl to remove it, she says. Then, depending whom you believe, the teacher either "brushed back" the fabric or "forcibly removed it."

5 **2** "That's my hijab!" the girl cried out, she told her mom later. Her hair was briefly exposed. Herman says she apologized and assumed the incident would blow over. She was wrong.

3 Within days, a Change.org petition called for Herman to be fired; it eventually collected more than 41,000 signatures. NBC News, *USA Today* and *the New York Times* carried the 10 story far beyond this New Jersey suburb.

4 The local prosecutor opened an investigation. The school district touted upcoming anti-bias training for the staff. "We are hopeful and all agree that the alleged actions of one employee should not condemn an entire community," the superintendent said in another statement.

15 **5** More than a year later, Tamar Herman remains barred from the classroom, cut off from

the calling and colleagues she loved. The school district is paying her not to teach. She is still terrified by threats from strangers on the internet, she says. Multiple lawsuits have been filed, and the issue has divided this suburban community along racial and religious lines.

CD2-16

20 **6** On the afternoon of Oct. 6, 2021, Cassandra Wyatt picked up her girls from school and headed to Dunkin' for an afternoon treat. As she was talking on the phone, she noticed her 7-year-old, Sumayyah, tugging on her arm, trying to get her attention. Finally, she looked down and listened.

7 "My teacher pulled my hijab off my head," Sumayyah told her mom, Wyatt said. Wyatt
25 wasn't sure whether to believe her and called another mom in the class, who was driving home with her own daughter. Wyatt heard the other girl's response from the back seat of their car. "Oh yeah, the teacher pulled off her hijab."

8 The next day, Wyatt logged onto Facebook. "Hi I am new to this group," she wrote on a page called SOMA Justice, which is devoted to issues of race and inequality in the area.
30 "My daughter told me that her teacher took her Hijab off her head and said she can't wear this in school in front of her class." In this telling, the teacher didn't just make a mistake. She acted purposefully.

9 Soon, someone — Wyatt said she can't remember who — messaged her that Herman is Jewish. On Facebook, she shared her views about this discovery: "SHES JEWISH!"
35 Wyatt wrote on the SOMA Justice page. "I JUST FOUND OUT THE TEACHER IS JEWISHHHHHHHHHH … that's why I believe she did it now I'm furious."

10 Asked about these comments, Wyatt said she meant that Herman should have understood the sensitivity of the hijab, since observant Jews also wear religious garb. But, she added, "I think that she's racist. I think she's anti-Muslim." The Wyatt family is
40 Black. Later, she amended her comments to say she wasn't sure if Herman was racist or anti-Muslim.

11 Joseph Wyatt, her then-husband, also pinned Herman's actions on her religion. "They think they're chosen by God," he said. "They come with the money. They run a lot of stuff. It's all Jewish names."

CD2-17

45 **12** It took less than a day for word of what happened in Tamar Herman's classroom to reach Ibtihaj Muhammad, an Olympic fencer who graduated from the South Orange-

Maplewood, N.J., school district. Muhammad made international headlines for competing in her hijab in 2016.

13 Muhammed posted unsparingly about the classroom incident on her Instagram and Facebook accounts, where she has hundreds of thousands of followers. "Imagine being a child and stripped of your clothing in front of your classmates," she wrote. "This is abuse." She named Herman and tagged CAIR, an Islamic civil rights group, which responded the next day by calling for Herman to be fired immediately.

14 Herman and Muhammad knew each other. They worked out together at the same gym and had each other's cellphone numbers. Herman had asked Muhammad to speak at her school, and the pair were friends on Facebook. Herman couldn't believe that Muhammad would post about her without first checking in or asking what happened. She texted the fencer. "I considered you a friend," she wrote, asking Muhammad to take the post down. "Not only is it 100% untrue, it was very hurtful to read."

CD2-18

15 On the day of the hijab incident, Tamar Herman had been a teacher for more than 30 years, including about 20 at Seth Boyden Elementary School, a stately brick structure set in the least wealthy part of town.

16 Herman spent her career incorporating diverse faiths and cultures into her teaching, her attorneys said. She gave a lesson featuring a girl in a hijab. She had a collection of appreciative notes and emails from parents and positive evaluations, including one that said she created a "climate and culture" of "respect and learning."

17 From her telling, the incident with Sumayyah Wyatt was an unfortunate misunderstanding. When the principal called her in the next day to ask what happened, Herman told her that as soon as she realized she'd pulled down a hijab and not a hoodie, "she immediately pulled it back and said sorry," according to a district incident report.

18 From the start, she had her defenders, and with time, her allies began to speak out more forcefully. A friend and former colleague, Alice Solomon, addressed the January 2022 school board meeting. She said Herman was a gentle person who could never have done what she was accused of. Solomon also asked that the district address the antisemitism connected to the case. "Maybe, as seen on so many lawn signs, maybe hate has no home here, but it sure does on the internet," she concluded.

19 A letter submitted to the school district in February 2022 by members of the community asked for officials to acknowledge and renounce the antisemitism "that has surfaced in the course of the campaign against Ms. Herman." Herman also questioned in a legal filing why the school district had spoken out in response to allegations of Islamophobia but not antisemitism.

20 Early last year, Cassandra Wyatt showed up at Herman's door unannounced, Herman said. According to Herman, the mom told her that her daughter loves Herman, wishing she were still her teacher. It was all a misunderstanding, the mom told her, Herman recalled.

21 In the Wyatts' case against Herman and the district, the parties reached a settlement of $295,000, and after some drama and demands for more, the Wyatts said this week that they will accept it. Sumayyah and her sister no longer attend the public schools. After the incident, Cassandra Wyatt moved their daughters to an Islamic school, their father's preference all along.

1,126 words

By Laura Meckler, March 1, 2023, *The Washington Post*

Notes

ℓ.29 SOMA Justice「ソーマ・ジャスティス」：
ニュージャージー州サウスオレンジ―メープルウッド学区（SOMA）に通う子どもたちの保護者によって作られたボランティアグループで、学区における人種的正義と、有色人種のための安全な空間づくりを促進するために活動している。2016年設立。

ℓ.46 Ibtihaj Muhammad「イブティハージ・ムハンマド（1985-）」：
アメリカ合衆国のフェンシング選手。2016年のリオ五輪で、アメリカ人女性として初めてヒジャブをつけて出場したことで話題になった（同大会ではフェンシング女子サーベル団体戦で銅メダルを獲得）。その後、彼女をモデルにしたヒジャブ姿のバービー人形が発売され、自身の体験をふまえてイスラム女性にとってのヒジャブの意義を書いた児童書 The Proudest Blue: A Story of Hijab and Family はベストセラーとなる。

ℓ.52 CAIR「アメリカ・イスラム関係評議会」：
正式名称は Council on American-Islamic Relations。アメリカ合衆国最大のイスラム教市民団体。国内のイスラム教徒の人権を守り、社会や政治、法律に関する活動促進を目的としている。

ℓ.74 antisemitism「反ユダヤ主義」：
ユダヤ人及びユダヤ教に対する嫌悪や偏見、迫害をさす。ルーツは古代に遡るが、1948年のイスラエル建国後は中東のイスラム諸国でもユダヤ人に対する嫌悪感が高まった。

ℓ.80 Islamophobia「イスラム恐怖症」：
イスラム教やイスラム教徒（ムスリム）に対して極度の恐怖を感じる症状全般をさす。

ℓ.85 the Wyatts' case against Herman and the district：
本記事にあるように、ワイアット夫妻がハーマンとSOMAを訴えた裁判では、295,000ドル（約4,000万円）という破格の和解金で和解が成立。和解金は3分の1が母親に、3分の1が父親に渡り、残りの3分の1が当事者の娘スマヤの信託へ預けられるという。これとは別に、ハーマン側も同学区や、イブティハージ・ムハンマド選手を名誉毀損で訴えている。

True or **F**alse | 英文を読んで、本文と合致する場合は T を、合致しない場合は F を記入しましょう。

1. Contrary to Herman's expectations, the incident developed into nationwide news. [   ]

2. Thanks to her colleagues' defense and support, Herman could go back to work about a year after the incident. [   ]

3. Herman knew Ibtihaj Muhammad, but they had never met in person. [   ]

4. Before the incident, Herman had a good reputation as a school teacher who promoted understanding diverse cultures and faiths in class. [   ]

5. The case hasn't been settled yet since Herman and the girl's mother are still fighting in court. [   ]

Question & **A**nswer | 次の質問に英文で答えましょう。

1. What did Cassandra Wyatt believe to be the reason Herman pushed back their daughter's hijab right after she received a message on social media?

_____

2. How did CAIR react to Muhammed's post?

_____

3. What did Alice Solomon request at the district meeting?

_____

Correction & **L**istening | 以下は5箇所の文法上の誤りを含んだ記事の要約文です。誤りを正しく直しましょう。その後、正しい音声を聞いて答えを確認しましょう。

◎ CD2-19

When a Jewish teacher named Tamar Herman pulled back her Muslim student's hijab, it lead to a series of events that ended in Herman being suspended and subject to threats involved the student's family, the Wyatts, the school and it's district, the court, and tens thousands of people on social media. The Wyatt's case against Herman and the district reached a settlement of $295,000, but that was not the only outcome; it also highlighted the public's sensitive reactions to difference religions and people's mistakes.

Reflecting on the Whole Article

とある学区内で起きた出来事が、やがてアメリカ全土のニュースへと発展したことは、SNS時代の情報伝達やリテラシー教育、そして多様な人種や宗教が共存することの難しさを物語っている。本記事は、複数の視点から一つの出来事を多角的に検証しており、事件の真相に迫る様子を立体的に表現しながら臨場感を最大限に引き出している。

 以下は記事全体の流れと、キーとなる英文です。ペアまたはグループを作り、これらの英文を読んで感じたことをシェアしましょう。その後、各メンバーで分担して次の質問について考え、答えを発表し合いましょう。

Paragraphs 1 – 5

ある小学校での出来事――先生が生徒のヒジャブを取るように指示?

Herman says she apologized and assumed the incident would blow over. She was wrong.

Q Why had she assumed this, and why was she wrong?

Paragraphs 6 – 11

生徒の両親側の視点――先生がユダヤ人と知った母親は……

… "I think that she's racist. I think she's anti-Muslim." (Cassandra Wyatt)

Q Do you think the mother truly believed the statement that she made? Why or Why not?

Paragraphs 12 – 14

ある有名アスリートの視点――事件の火に油をそそぐ

"Not only is it 100% untrue, it was very hurtful to read." (Tamar Herman)

Q Other than Muhammad posting things that are not true, what else about Muhammad's reaction might hurt Herman's feeling?

Paragraphs 15 – 21

先生の視点と事件の真相、その後の顛末

From the start, she had her defenders, and with time, her allies began to speak out more forcefully.

Q What positive point did these defenders make about Herman?

Discussing the Issues

日本でもSNS上でデマやバッシングが横行し、問題になっている。以下は、本章の記事に寄せられたコメントである。

 Posting Your Comment | 次のコメントを参考に、あなた自身の意見を書いてみましょう。

Liz, *6 hours ago*
It's unfortunate that no one properly checked the truth and a small misunderstanding turned into a heated dispute that led to the removal of a good educator from the school district.

Angie, *3 hours ago*
Was this a simple mistake or a case of religious discrimination? Why didn't Muhammad contact Herman directly to verify the facts?

Live&learn, *2 hours ago*
Why did Wyatt post her views on social media first before checking with Herman? People need to understand the power of social media.

You, *now*

_____

_____

_____

 Window to Further Research

偽情報や相手を貶めようとする情報は、SNSやメディアなどにより瞬時に大量配信され、拡散し、社会の分断にもつながり得る。さまざまな情報が蔓延する時代を生きる私たちは、相手を正しく理解し、受け取った情報を客観的に受け止める努力をする必要があるだろう。イスラム教や、情報の受け止め方について知見を深められる文献を紹介する。

 『イスラーム思想を読みとく』
松山洋平著、筑摩書房、2017年
一神教であるイスラム教の全体像や過激派と他のイスラム教徒との違い、それぞれの宗派の思想構造や特徴について具体的で分かりやすく解説しているイスラム教の入門書である。

 The Misinformation Age: How False Beliefs Spread
by Cailin O'Connor & James Owen Weatherall,
Yale University Press, 2020
筆者はさまざまなケーススタディに触れながら、誤った情報の広がりを正しく理解するには、その情報の性質とそれが広まる社会システムの両方を考える必要があると主張する。

The Guardian

Basic Information

創立 1821年
創業者 ジョン・エドワード・テイラーほか
形態 日刊紙
本社 イギリス・ロンドン
姉妹媒体
The Observer（日曜発刊）、
The Guardian Weekly（国際向けの週刊誌）

200年以上の歴史をもつイギリスを代表する高級紙。1821年に「マンチェスター・ガーディアン」という名でマンチェスターを拠点にスタート。当初から中道左派、リベラル寄りのスタンスを打ち出し、1872年から編集長を務めたチャールズ・プレスウィッチ・スコット（1907年に会社を買収し社主を兼務）の手腕もあり有力紙へと発展した。

1959年に現在の「ガーディアン」に変更後、1964年に本社をロンドンに移した。スコットの死後は息子がスコット・トラストという財団を立ち上げ、所有権も移転させた。トラストの目的は同紙の「財政的・編集的独立性を永続的に確保すること」「商業的・政治的干渉から報道の自由とリベラルな価値を守る」ことで、利益は所有者や株主に分配されるのではなく、ジャーナリズムに再投資される。その方針は有限会社になった今でも変わらない。なお、有力紙の中ではデジタル記事をすべて無料で閲覧できる稀有な存在だが、ジャーナリズムの独立性を保つために読者からの寄付を積極的に呼びかけている。その結果、2020年にはデジタルの有料読者数が100万人を突破し、2022-23年の決算では総収入の70%をデジタルでの収益が占めるようになった。

政府の圧力もかわして報道を続けた
名物編集長の英断──「スノーデン文書」

2013年6月、同紙はアメリカの国家安全保障局（NSA）の契約社員エドワード・スノーデンが入手した同組織の内部文書を立て続けに公開した。文書によれば、当時の米オバマ政権がテロ対策の名目で一般市民の通話やEメールを傍受してきたこと、またイギリスの政府通信本部（GCHQ）と協力し、国際電話やインターネットを通じて世界中の組織や市民を監視している実態が明らかになった。この報道は国際問題に発展し、更なる暴露を危惧した英政府はGCHQの職員2名をガーディアン本社に送り、スノーデン文書が入ったハードディスク全てを破壊させた。しかし、当時の編集長アラン・ラスブリッジャーの判断で事前にコピーがアメリカ支社に送られており（ちなみに、彼はこのことも事前に当局に伝えている）、以後もUS版から公開を続けた（アメリカを選んだのは報道の自由を認めた憲法修正第1条があるので国家権力が手を出しにくいという彼の判断によるもの）。この一連の報道により、同紙は2014年のピュリツァー賞をワシントン・ポストと共同で受賞した。

Stories
of The World We Live In

IV

SURVIVE

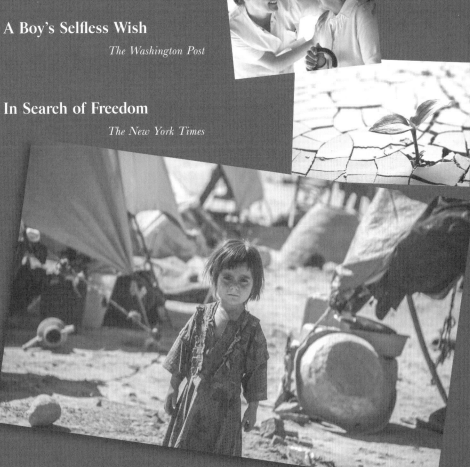

Chapter 9

A Boy's Selfless Wish

The Washington Post

What is on your bucket list of things to do before you die? If you could wish for anything in the world, what would it be?

_____

Vocabulary Sorting

次の語句をカテゴリーに分類しましょう。未知語はペアで意味を確認しましょう。

disorder	active	brush off	unwell
transplant	anemia	bubbly	boundless energy
good spirits	eyes watered	goose bumps	philanthropic
selfless	charitable	rally around	

Health issue	Altruism (Opposite to selfishness)	Emotional / Physical reaction	Personality / Mood
•	•	•	•
•	•	•	•
•	•	•	•
•	•	•	•

Words in Context

日本語のヒントを参考に、上の語句から適切な表現を選び、必要な場合は文に合うように形を変えて空欄に記入しましょう。　　🔘 CD2-20

Children are often **1.** _____, finding it difficult to sit still. Playing
<small>活発な</small>
with each other, often energetically, keeps them in **2.** _____. If a child
<small>上機嫌</small>
is constantly tired, parents may **3.** _____ the symptoms, but it is possible the
<small>無視する</small>
child has **4.** _____. In such cases, the family must **5.** _____ and
<small>貧血</small> <small>味方になる</small>
do everything they can to help. The case of Abraham Olagbegi shows how a sick child
who is **6.** _____, thinking only of others, can inspire us all even when that child is
<small>私欲がない</small>
7. _____.
<small>調子がよくない</small>

Reading the Article

 CD2-21

Many Make-A-Wish kids ask for a vacation. This teen asked to feed the homeless

1 Abraham Olagbegi is 13 and has a rare blood disorder. On the way home from a doctor's appointment in July, his mother, who had just learned that her son qualified as a Make-A-Wish recipient, asked him what he might want.

2 "If you could wish for anything in the world, what would it be?" Miriam Olagbegi
5 asked him. He could have asked for a PlayStation, a shopping spree or a trip to Disneyland, but there was only one thing he felt strongly about. "I really want to feed the homeless," he said.

3 His mom was momentarily surprised. "But when I think about the kind of kid he is, his answer made perfect sense," said Olagbegi, who lives in Jackson, Miss. Together, they

10 filled out the Make-A-Wish application, which asks recipients to outline their wish and their reasons for wanting it to come true. Children between the ages of 2 and 18 who suffer from a critical illness are eligible for a wish.

4 "I would like for the homeless people at Poindexter Park in Jackson to receive one hot meal a month every month for the rest of the year or for an entire year," Abraham wrote

15 on the form. He explained his reasoning behind his wish: "Before I got sick, me and my family would go feed the homeless at that park every month. Since I became sick, my family had to stop doing it. I really want to do something impactful."

5 Abraham said he didn't have to think hard about what to wish for. The decision, he said, was "second nature." "My mom would always say it's a blessing to be a blessing,"

20 Abraham said in an interview with *The Washington Post*.

CD2-22

6 It was nearly a year and a half ago, in June 2020, when Abraham's world suddenly slammed to a halt. He had always been healthy, his mother said, but that spring, Olagbegi and her husband started to notice subtle changes in their son's stamina and overall demeanor. They brushed it off, assuming he had overexerted himself or was simply

25 overtired.

7 The situation escalated when Abraham woke up in the middle of the night, feeling unwell. He fainted in the hallway on his way to his parents' bedroom. An ambulance rushed Abraham to the hospital, where he was immediately taken to the emergency room. He underwent tests to determine the cause of his sudden malaise.

30 **8** His doctors soon discovered that he had aplastic anemia, a rare and life-threatening condition that occurs when the body does not produce enough new blood cells. He would require a bone-marrow transplant. Abraham went from being a bubbly, active child with boundless energy to a weak, fragile boy confined to a hospital bed. Despite his diagnosis, though, "I try to always keep good spirits and think about the positive," said Abraham,

35 who carried on with his schoolwork remotely during his nine months of treatment — one month of which was spent in the hospital.

9 Beyond attending school and playing basketball with his friends, what Abraham missed the most while he was in the hospital, he said, was feeding the homeless — a regular ritual that he and his family did together. In fact, the day he was admitted to the hospital, he

40 looked over at his mother and said: "Mama, does this mean I won't get to go and feed the homeless anymore?"

10 For the past four years, Abraham's family has been feeding the homeless in their community in Jackson once a month. His great-uncle started the family tradition of cooking together and providing hot meals to those in need. "Abraham just really took a
45 liking to it. He is always eager to make sure he goes," Olagbegi said. "He loves just serving personally."

CD2-23

11 After his doctors referred him as a recipient to Make-A-Wish Mississippi, Abraham knew he wanted to use his wish to carry on his family's mission of feeding those in need. When Linda Sermons, a wish assistant at Make-A-Wish Mississippi, opened Abraham's
50 paperwork with her manager, "our eyes watered up and we got goose bumps," she said, adding that Abraham's wish is the Mississippi chapter's first philanthropic request. "It was a milestone for us. His wish is selfless."

12 Top wish requests include a trip to Disney World, an international vacation, a bedroom makeover and meeting a celebrity. Some wishes are entirely unique — an 8-year-old girl
55 with leukemia, for example, wished to become a mother for a day — while charitable wishes like Abraham's are very rare. "Abraham has been an inspiration to us all," said Allison Tyler, the chief executive of Make-A-Wish Mississippi. "Hundreds of wishes get granted every day across the nation, but being part of his touches the heart."

13 The nonprofit organization committed to grant Abraham's wish, vowing to feed at least
60 80 homeless people at Poindexter Park on every third Saturday of each month for a full year. The food for the monthly event, which it decided to call "Abraham's Table," is supplied by various donors and sponsors, including local churches and businesses.

14 "This wish is definitely leaving a mark, not only because of the milestone it gave our chapter, but also meeting this family and knowing how the community can truly rally
65 around our kids is just amazing," Sermons said. The first two events, Sept. 18 and Oct. 16, were a success, and for Abraham, the best part was "seeing the look on everybody's faces," he said. "It just really warms my heart."

CD2-24

15 Abraham's condition has continued to improve in recent months, and while he is still unable to attend school because his immune system is compromised, his doctors are

70 hopeful that he'll be back in class in a few months. Although his blood disorder is not fatal, "it's something that's going to impact him forever," Olagbegi said. "He will always have to be careful when he's out in public around people."

16 He and his family plan to continue Abraham's Table, even after the final event organized by Make-A-Wish is held in August. "We are hoping to one day get food trucks," Abraham
75 explained, adding that he wants to turn Abraham's Table into a nonprofit organization. For now, though, Abraham feels fulfilled. "My wish has definitely come true," he said.

1,029 words

By Sydney Page, Nov. 16, 2021, *The Washington Post*

Notes

ℓ.3 Make-A-Wish「メイク・ア・ウィッシュ」:
1980年にアメリカ・アリゾナ州で活動を開始した非営利団体で、現在は日本を含む世界約50カ国に支部を持つ。難病を持つ子どもの夢の実現を手伝うことを主な目的とする。

ℓ.9 Jackson「ジャクソン」:
アメリカ・ミシシッピ州の州都で、州最大の都市。南北戦争(1861-1865)では激戦地として多大な戦禍を被った。地名は南北戦争で活躍し、のちに第7代アメリカ合衆国大統領になったアンドリュー・ジャクソンに因む。

ℓ.30 aplastic anemia「再生不良性貧血」:
骨髄が十分な数の新しい血球(赤血球、白血球、血小板)を作らなくなる病気。日本でも難病に指定され、年間約1,000人が発症している。

ℓ.61 Abraham's Table「エイブラハムの食卓」:
エイブラハムが立ち上げたホームレスのための炊き出しイベントはメイク・ア・ウィッシュ財団のサポートが終了したあともクラウドファンディングで資金を募り、不定期で継続している。
→ www.gofundme.com/f/abrahams-table

True or **F**alse | 英文を読んで、本文と合致する場合は T を、合致しない場合は F を記入しましょう。

1. When Abraham wished to feed the homeless as an eligible Make-A-Wish recipient, his mother didn't understand where his idea came from. [   ]

2. At first, Abraham's symptoms seemed mild, but they worsened to the point that he required transplant surgery. [   ]

3 Feeding the homeless was a big part of the Olagbegi family's tradition that Abraham had always hoped to take part in but never had a chance to. [   ]

4. Abraham's wish was inspiring for the Make-A-Wish staff and touched their hearts. [   ]

5. "Abraham's Table" was realized through the cooperation of various supporters and became a landmark event for Make-A-Wish. [   ]

Question & **A**nswer | 次の質問に英文で答えましょう。

1. What kind of person is qualified as a Make-A-Wish recipient?

_____

2. What kind of disease is aplastic anemia?

_____

3. What do Make-A-Wish applicants usually wish for?

_____

Correction & **L**istening | 以下は 5 箇所の文法上の誤りを含んだ記事の要約文です。誤りを正しく直しましょう。その後、正しい音声を聞いて答えを確認しましょう。

 CD2-25

　　Abraham Olagbegi is a teenager lived in Jackson, Mississippi, who was diagnosed with aplastic anemia. He qualified as a Make-A-Wish recipient. Despite many children wish for video games, shopping, or a memorable trip, Abraham's wish was to provide one hot meal to the homeless people in his neighborhood. This was a family tradition that he missed much than anything while he was in hospitalized. The organization was inspired by Abraham's selfless wish. Abraham's wish was granted, and he is now moving forward his next dream of making a nonprofit organization to feed the homeless.

Reflecting on the Whole Article

本章の記事は、自身も病気を抱えているにもかかわらずホームレスの人々の助けになろうとする少年の利他の心がコミュニティの中で広がり、慈善プロジェクトを動かす大きな力へと発展していくさまを伝えている。本人や関係者が当時の気持ちを吐露した発言を多く引用することで、記事全体が感情の乗った生き生きとしたものに仕上がっている。

 以下は記事全体の流れと、キーとなる英文です。ペアまたはグループを作り、これらの英文を読んで感じたことをシェアしましょう。その後、各メンバーで分担して次の質問について考え、答えを発表し合いましょう。

Paragraphs **1** — **5**

「ホームレスに食事を」——エイブラハムの願いの背景にあるもの

His [Abraham's] mom was momentarily surprised. "But when I think about the kind of kid he is, his answer made perfect sense"

Ⓠ In his mother's opinion, what kind of child is Abraham?

Paragraphs **6** — **10**

エイブラハムの生活を一変させた病と家族の伝統行事への想い

"Mama, does this mean I won't get to go and feed the homeless anymore?"
(Abraham Olagbegi)

Ⓠ What does "this" mean here?

Paragraphs **11** — **14**

エイブラハムの想いがMake-A-Wish側の心も動かす

"Hundreds of wishes get granted every day across the nation, but being part of his touches the heart." (Allison Tyler, the chief executive of Make-A-Wish Mississippi)

Ⓠ Why was Abraham's wish special for her?

Paragraphs **15** — **16**

願いの実現を経て、エイブラハムが未来に想うことは……

He [Abraham] and his family plan to continue Abraham's Table, ...

Ⓠ What are Abraham's plans for the future?

Discussing the Issues

ボランティアや寄付といった慈善活動のやり方については色々な見方がある。以下は本章の記事に寄せられたコメントである。

 Posting Your Comment | 次のコメントを参考に、あなた自身の意見を書いてみましょう。

George Dent, *7 hours ago*
Abraham's selfless wish is truly an inspiration to others, but wouldn't the donations be better spent on research into curing these terrible diseases that afflict children? That would lead to the "greatest happiness of the greatest number."

Painfree, *3 hours ago*
Make-A-Wish brings hope to so many. We should do everything we can for these sick children. How about expanding the program so that every child gets their wish, not only the lucky few who are chosen?

Blessings-2-u, *2 hours ago*
I heard some people do charity for their own benefit, such as avoiding taxes. Even so, personally, I think taking action is way better than doing nothing. What do you think?

You, *now*

_____

_____

_____

 Window to Further Research

貧困や戦争、災害などによって住まいを失った人々は世界で1億5,000人にのぼるといわれ、ホームレスは世界的な社会問題のひとつである。このような問題を支援する人々の強い想いと行動は、そのコミュニティにも大きな影響力をもたらす。このテーマについて理解を深めるためには以下の文献がおすすめである。

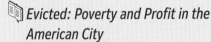📖 *Evicted: Poverty and Profit in the American City*
by Matthew Desmond, Crown, 2016
アメリカ貧困地域で家賃の支払いに苦労している8家族を対象とした1年間の民族学的フィールドワークによって、貧困の原因、住宅状況、経済的搾取などアメリカの社会問題を浮き彫りにしている。2017年、ピュリツァー賞を受賞。

📖 *Once Upon A Wish: True Inspirational Stories of Make-A-Wish Children*
by Rachelle Sparks & Frank Shankwitz, BenBella Books, 2013
Make-A-Wish財団の創設者らによって書かれた、これまでの活動の記録。病院に多額の寄付をすることを生涯の目標とした少女など、8人の子どもたちとその家族の物語を通して、願いを叶えることがいかに人々に希望や勇気を与え、人生の動機づけとなるかを提唱する。

Chapter
10

In Search of Freedom

The New York Times

What conditions would cause you to leave your own country? In such a case, what country would you choose to flee to?

Vocabulary **S**orting | 次の語句をカテゴリーに分類しましょう。未知語はペアで意味を確認しましょう。

anti-government	conscript	imprisoned	flee
dissident	asylum	activist	refuge
exodus	assault	detained	incarcerated
injure	bloodshed	hunger strike	custody

Protest	War	Captivity	Escape
•	•	•	•
•	•	•	•
•	•	•	•
•	•	•	•

Words in **C**ontext | 日本語のヒントを参考に、上の語句から適切な表現を選び、必要な場合は文に合うように形を変えて空欄に記入しましょう。　　 CD2-26

　　When people **1.** _____ from authoritarian regimes, they may claim **2.** _____
　　　　　　　　　　　逃げる　　　　　　　　　　　　　　　　　　　　　　　　　　　　　　　　　　　亡命
in a democratic state. Some of these people posted videos of the **3.** _____ on
　　　流血の（惨事）
social media and became the victims of **4.** _____. When countries are torn apart
　　　　　　　　　　　　　　　　　　　　　　　　　　　　　攻撃
by war, there is a great **5.** _____ of refugees. These people may be detained at the
　　　　　　　　　　　　　　大移動
border or even held in **6.** _____ for extended periods.
　　　　　　　　　　　　拘留

Reading the Article

 CD2-27

Antiwar activists who flee Russia find detention, not freedom, in the U.S.

1 They had fallen in love their first year in medical school in Russia, joined by their commitment to building democracy in a country where any remaining hope of it was disappearing.

2 When Russia pushed into Ukraine, Mariia Shemiatina and Boris Shevchuk, who had
5 married and become practicing physicians, posted videos of the bloodshed and antiwar messages on social media. "I call on Russians to see the truth, to not believe the lies of the Russian media," Ms. Shemiatina, 29, wrote on Instagram. Her posts were deleted by the authorities again and again, she said — until her accounts were blocked.

3 The police called her family in search of the couple, who had gone into hiding. Certain
10 that they were on the brink of being conscripted to serve as medics on the front lines, or imprisoned for their political activity, the couple decided to flee.

 CD2-28

4 As Vladimir Putin cracks down on dissidents and arrests draft dodgers, growing numbers of Russians are making their way across the U.S. southern border. But contrary to their expectations of asylum and freedom, many of them are being put into immigration
15 detention centers that resemble prisons.

5 Even before Russia's assault on Ukraine, anti-government activists had been pouring out of the country and seeking refuge in the United States. The exodus intensified after the war began in late February, reaching the highest tallies in recent history. In the 2022 fiscal year, 21,763 Russians were processed by U.S. authorities at the southern border, compared with 467 in 2020. In October alone, 3,879 came.

6 Everyone who touches American soil has the right to claim asylum, though it is granted only to those who can prove they were persecuted in their home country based on their race, religion, nationality, political opinion or membership in a particular social group. Many asylum seekers are released and allowed to argue their cases later in court. But thousands are sent to detention centers, where it is difficult to secure lawyers and collect evidence, and the chances of winning asylum are extremely slim.

7 U.S. Immigration and Customs Enforcement (ICE) has not released statistics on the nationalities of migrants being held behind bars, but lawyers who work regularly with migrants say Russian asylum seekers appear to have been detained at relatively high rates in recent months — sometimes with bonds set in excess of $30,000. Some Russians have remained incarcerated for months under conditions they describe as extremely harsh.

8 Many said they had come to the United States thinking they would be welcomed as allies in America's push for democracy in Russia and Ukraine. Olga Nikitina, who fled Russia with her husband after he was imprisoned there multiple times, spent five months in Louisiana. "The whole time I was there, they treated us like garbage," said Ms. Nikitina, 33. "I called hotlines, but it did not help in any way." Her husband, Aleksandr Balashov, 33, was detained for four months at a facility in Batavia, N.Y., where he says officers told him and others that they had no rights because they had entered the country illegally.

⊙ CD2-29

9 Mr. Shevchuk and Ms. Shemiatina had been increasingly concerned about corruption and crackdowns on public expression in Russia. When Russia invaded Ukraine in late February, the couple began posting photos and videos on Instagram and V Kontakte, a Russian platform, and learned that the police were looking for them. As doctors were mobilized for the war effort, they decided they had to leave the country.

10 Unable to obtain visas to the European Union, they followed the route of other recent Russian dissidents, flying to Mexico on April 13. Two weeks later, in the city of Tijuana, they reached the U.S. border and requested protection.

11 At the port of entry near San Diego, when they were ordered to remove valuables, Mr.

Shevchuk tucked their wedding bands into a compartment of his backpack. After six days in separate, cold and windowless cells, they were flown to Louisiana on May 5 and placed in different detention centers.

12 After three weeks, Ms. Shemiatina had her first court appearance — over video with a judge thousands of miles away. She told her that she had illegally entered the country, but could assemble evidence to support her claim for asylum. Ms. Shemiatina explained that all the evidence was in the cellphone and laptop that authorities had confiscated, including screenshots of her antiwar posts, a notice about the call-up of physicians and evidence of threats she was receiving.

13 At Pine Prairie, Mr. Shevchuk went through similar motions. After a detainee threatened violence against him and other Russians, Mr. Shevchuk demanded they be moved. A guard handcuffed them during the transfer and knocked Mr. Shevchuk to the ground, he said, causing him to injure his head on the cement floor and his nose to bleed. "I came to realize that I had left Russia for a place that was just like Russia," he said.

14 Mr. Shevchuk went on a hunger strike. He fired off complaints to the immigration detention ombudsman, hotlines for human rights groups and the U.N. High Commissioner for Refugees.

15 Their lawyer, Jessica Gutierrez, filed requests for the couple's release, noting that they were not a flight risk. ICE responded that "after review of all the relevant facts," it had determined that they could be released if each posted bond in the amount of $15,000. But where would they find $30,000?

16 By then, Ms. Shemiatina had begun experiencing excruciating pain in her pelvic area and numbness on the left side of her body, but M.R.I.s were inconclusive, according to medical reports reviewed by *the Times*. On Oct. 5, she was found unconscious in her room and then began having seizures. She was taken by ambulance to a nearby hospital, where doctors diagnosed her with an unspecified neurological problem. When she was unable to walk without assistance, Ms. Gutierrez demanded her immediate release from ICE custody to "preserve her life." Instead, she was sent back to detention.

17 On Oct. 28, ICE agreed to lower the bond for the couple to $10,000 each — money they still did not have. Finally, a Russian dissident Mr. Shevchuk had met at the border, Mr. Balashov, amassed the money to free Ms. Shemiatina.

18 Dan Gashler, a history professor at the State University of New York in Delhi and a
volunteer for Freedom for Immigrants, which aids detained immigrants, had organized
a fund-raiser to pay Mr. Shevchuk's bond and fly the couple to New York. Community
members volunteered to house and help them. "These are incredible young people who
fled because of their opposition to the regime," he said, "and fell victim to our broken
asylum process."

19 On Nov. 8, Ms. Shemiatina climbed into a minivan, her lawyer at the wheel, for the three-
hour drive to meet her husband at Pine Prairie. "I'm more happy than on my wedding day,"
she declared. When Mr. Shevchuk emerged from the concertina-ringed facility, smiling
broadly, he quickened his pace to reunite with his wife, who hobbled toward him. From
his backpack, Mr. Shevchuk retrieved the wedding band he had hidden away six months
earlier. He slipped it on Ms. Shemiatina's finger.

1,182 words

By Miriam Jordan, Nov. 28, 2022, *The New York Times*

Notes

ℓ.12 growing numbers of Russians are making their way across the U.S. southern border：
2022年2月のロシアによるウクライナ侵攻後、侵攻に反対する多くのロシア人が国外へ出国した。
特に同年9月に予備役の部分的動員令が発令された後に、その数がさらに増加した。多くはジョー
ジアやアルメニアなど旧ソ連の構成国へと「一時的な」避難をする一方で、本文のマリアとボリ
ス夫妻のように祖国に見切りをつけて亡命するパターンも少なくない。

ℓ.27 U.S. Immigration and Customs Enforcement (ICE)「アメリカ合衆国移民・関税執行局」:
米国連邦政府の移民法と関税法を執行する機関で、主に入国管理やテロの防止、違法な移動の
取り締まりなどを行う。ロシア国内で弾圧される恐れのある難民申請者に対する非人道的な応
対は批判を浴びたが、さらに2023年には、侵攻後は取りやめていたロシアへの強制送還措置を
密かに再開し、上記のような人々をロシアへ強制送還させていたことが判明した。

ℓ.41 V Kontakte「フ コンタクテ」:
ロシア版フェイスブックとも呼ばれる同国最大のSNSで、暗号化メッセージアプリ、テレグラム
(Telegram)の生みの親でもあるパーヴェル・ドゥーロフが2006年に立ち上げた。現在は国営
企業VKグループが運営している。ウクライナ侵攻後の2022年9月、Appleはフ コンタクテを含む、
VKグループのアプリをApp Storeから削除した。

ℓ.63 U.N. High Commissioner for Refugees (UNHCR)「国連難民高等弁務官事務所」:
1950年に設立された、国際連合内の難民問題に取り組む機関。自国から迫害の恐れのある人々
が第三国の庇護を求めやすいように、また避難後に自国へ送還されないように国を跨いで調整
することが主な役割である。日本では1991年から10年間、緒方貞子氏が高等弁務官を務めたこ
とで認知されるようになった。ちなみに、難民認定率が著しく低い日本に対し、同事務所は間口
を広げるように度重ねて勧告している。

ℓ.80 Freedom for Immigrants「フリーダム・フォー・イミグランツ」:
全国的なホットラインとボランティアによる移民収容施設の訪問を通じ、収容所に拘禁された移
民に対する人権侵害を監視する非営利団体。2010年にクリスティーナ・フィアリョとクリスティーナ・
マンスフィールドによって設立された。

英文を読んで、本文と合致する場合はTを、合致しない場合はFを記入しましょう。

1. The number of Russians processed by the U.S. authorities at the southern border soared after Russia's assault on Ukraine. [   ]

2. On their arrival in the United States, the couple had all their belongings taken, including their wedding rings. [   ]

3. Ms. Shemiatina talked with the judge in person at her court appearance. [   ]

4. The couple could not pay the bonds that ICE initially required for their release. [   ]

5. Ms. Shemiatina was not released from ICE custody right away even after she developed a serious health problem. [   ]

 次の質問に英文で答えましょう。

1. Why did the couple decide to escape from Russia?

_____

2. What kind of people are granted the right to claim asylum in the United States?

_____

3. How did Dan Gashler support the couple?

_____

Correction & **L**istening 以下は5箇所の文法上の誤りを含んだ記事の要約文です。誤りを正しく直しましょう。その後、正しい音声を聞いて答えを確認しましょう。

🔘 CD2-31

When Russia invade Ukraine, a Russian couple was brave enough to send out antiwar messages in social media, but after receiving threats from the authorities, they decided to leaving the country. The couple fled to Mexico and reached to the U.S. border. However, upon arrival, they were subjected to six months of inhumane treatment in different detention centers. Experiencing violence and illness, they were fortunately to receive support from others and were finally able to reunite. More and more Russians are now seeking refuge in the United States in search of freedom, but freedom is not easy to come by.

Reflecting on the Whole Article

本記事は、一組のロシア人夫婦の体験を通して、人種・宗教・政治上のあらゆる弾圧から逃れてきた人の人権保護を保障するとされるアメリカ合衆国への亡命が、実際はいかに過酷で危険を伴い且つ狭き門であるかを克明に描写している。アメリカでの厳しい現実に直面し、ようやく解放された二人が再会に至るまでの試練に満ちた臨場感溢れる記事である。

 以下は記事全体の流れと、キーとなる英文です。ペアまたはグループを作り、これらの英文を読んで感じたことをシェアしましょう。その後、各メンバーで分担して次の質問について考え、答えを発表し合いましょう。

Paragraphs **1** — **3**

ロシア人夫婦の決断──反戦運動から亡命までの経緯

They had fallen in love their first year in medical school in Russia, joined by their commitment to building democracy in a country where any remaining hope of it was disappearing.

Q How did this couple try to build democracy in Russia, and what was the result?

Paragraphs **4** — **8**

増加するロシア人亡命希望者を待ち受けている厳しい現状

Everyone who touches American soil has the right to claim asylum, though it is granted only to those who can prove they were persecuted in their home country ...

Q What often happens to Russians who claim asylum in the United States?

Paragraphs **9** — **13**

出国後のロシア人夫婦を襲った悲劇──表現の自由を求める闘い、覚悟の亡命、夫婦の別離、拘置センターでの惨状

"I came to realize that I had left Russia for a place that was just like Russia"
(Boris Shevchuk)

Q What does Mr. Shevchuck mean by this? Include what he experienced in your answer.

Paragraphs **14** — **19**

結末はいかに──ストライキ、病気、周囲のサポート、そして再会

When Mr. Shevchuk emerged from the concertina-ringed facility, smiling broadly, he quickened his pace to reunite with his wife, who hobbled toward him.

Q Describe their feelings at this point.

Discussing the Issues

紛争や迫害などが原因で生まれ故郷を追われる人は、世界で1億人を超えるといわれている。以下は本章の記事についてのコメントである。

 Posting Your Comment | 次のコメントを参考に、あなた自身の意見を書いてみましょう。

Sora, *4 hours ago*
It seems refugees keep on increasing for reasons of war, political or religious persecution, and even the changing climate. I wish I knew how we could all share the idea that we are all part of this world and exist in the context of the whole.

Truepatriot, *3 hours ago*
I'm not unsympathetic to the plight of refugees and asylum seekers, but here's the truth of the matter: this country is full. We cannot keep accepting people ad infinitum.

Naomi, *2 hours ago*
It was shocking to learn that most asylum seekers are detained for so long under harsh conditions with very little hope of being granted asylum. Has it always been like this regardless of who's in charge in the U.S. government?

You, *now*

_____

_____

_____

 Window to Further Research | 国際移民の数は年々増加傾向にあるものの、日本は移民の受け入れ数が依然として少なく、戦争難民を含む移民法や収容所の待遇は国により大きく異なる。今一度民主主義とは、人権とは何か、そしてそれを守るためにはどんな政策が必要かについて考えたい。

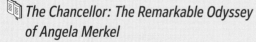

The Chancellor: The Remarkable Odyssey of Angela Merkel
by Kati Marton, William Collins, 2021
長期間、民主主義に基づく政策を貫いたドイツの元首相メルケルは、人道的理由から大量の難民を受け入れた。それは自由のない警察国家東ドイツで育ったメルケルの信念でもあったと言える。民主主義を考察するのに適した伝記。

The Ungrateful Refugee: What Immigrants Never Tell You
by Dina Nayeri, Catapult, 2019
8歳で家族とイランを脱出し、イタリアの難民キャンプで過ごした後にアメリカに亡命した著者が自身とその他の難民たちの体験について語る。また、欧米での難民政策にも一石を投じる。難民問題を理解するために適切な一冊。

THE NEW YORKER

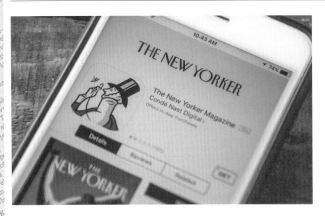

Basic Information

創立　　1925年

形態　　週刊誌

本社　　アメリカ合衆国ニューヨーク州

マスコットのシルクハット紳士

　紳士の名はユースタス・ティリー。創刊号で登場して以降、記念号や販促物などに使用され、雑誌のマスコット的存在に。

　ザ・ニューヨーカーは1925年にハロルド・ロスとその妻ジェーン・グラントによって創刊された。その名の通り、当初はニューヨーク近郊の読者を対象に、地元の娯楽や文化、社会生活を取り上げた雑誌だったが、徐々に時事問題や海外ルポルタージュ、文学、エッセイなど広範囲になり、ウィットとユーモアに溢れ、都会的に洗練された雑誌として世界中に読者を獲得した。特に文学においてはトルーマン・カポーティやJ.D.サリンジャーなど名だたる作家が寄稿し、同誌に掲載されることが作家としてのステータスとなった。1990年に初めて短編が掲載された村上春樹は「僕にとっては、おおげさに言えば、『月面を歩く』のと同じくらいすごいことだった。どんな文学賞をもらうよりも嬉しかった」とのちに書いている。だが、後述するように同誌は歴史に残る画期的な調査報道も多く残している。

　1951年の死まで編集長を続けたロスの死後も一族が経営していたが、現在は多国籍メディアコングロマリットのコンデナストがオーナーである。2014年（他誌より比較的早い時期）に同誌の有料デジタル化を開始し、当初は9万部弱のデジタル購買部数が2021年には35万部超と約4倍に。雑誌のDX成功例のさきがけとなっている。

社会問題を鋭くえぐる調査報道の歴史 ——「ヒロシマ」「沈黙の春」ほか

　1946年春、従軍記者で作家でもあったジョン・ハーシーは同誌から派遣されて広島を訪れた。原爆投下から1年も経っていない同地の悲惨な状況に驚愕しつつ、彼は人間に焦点を当て原爆の惨状を記録する。このルポはそれまで原爆の影響をほとんど知らされていなかったアメリカ国民の大きな反響を呼んだ。

　殺虫剤や農薬が身体や地球環境に及ぼす悪影響を科学的に検証し、その後の環境運動に大きな影響を与えたレイチェル・カーソンの「沈黙の春」※も最初は同誌に 3 回の連載記事として掲載された（1962年）。

　また近年では、先述したニューヨーク・タイムズと同時期にハーヴェイ・ワインスタインのセクハラ疑惑を追い、同紙の記者二人と一緒にピュリツァー賞を受賞したローナン・ファローによる調査報道記事がある。

※ 同書は Chapter 12 でも紹介（113ページ）

Stories
of The World We Live In

V

SUSTAIN

Chapter 11

Global Warming Solutions from the Past

The Washington Post

Have you ever thought how climate change has started to affect our planet? Do you know ancient wisdom may help solve it?

V^{ocabulary} S^{orting}

次の語句をカテゴリーに分類しましょう。未知語はペアで意味を確認しましょう。

shield	monsoon	passive water harvesting	squash
desert	parched	dryland	crop
precipitation	edible plant	seed bank	drought
60-day corn	irrigation	lowland	

Weather	Agricultural produce	Agricultural technique/ strategy	Geographical area
•	•	•	•
•	•	•	•
•	•	•	•
•	•	•	

W^{ords in} C^{ontext}

日本語のヒントを参考に、上の語句から適切な表現を選び、必要な場合は文に合うように形を変えて空欄に記入しましょう。 ⊙ CD3-02

Native Americans encountered various **1.** _____, ranging from mountainous
　　　　　　　　　　　　　　　　　　　　　　　　乾燥地
areas to **2.** _____ deserts. Over the millennia, they became experts at adaptation.
　　　　　　干上がった
For example, in desert regions, where there was little **3.** _____, they
　　　　　　　　　　　　　　　　　　　　　　　　　　　　　　　　　　　　降水
cultivated plants resistant to **4.** _____ and used advanced **5.** _____
　　　　　　　　　　　　　　　　　　干ばつ　　　　　　　　　　　　　　　　　　　　　灌漑
techniques. The first English settlers relied on the ancestral knowledge of the indigenous
people to cultivate the **6.** _____ that provided the food they needed. The
　　　　　　　　　　　　　　　　　食用植物
7. _____ they harvested helped keep them alive in the early years.
　　　収穫物

Reading the Article

 CD3-03

Native Americans' farming practices may help feed a warming world

1 TUCSON — Indigenous peoples have known for millennia to plant under the shade of the mesquite and paloverde trees that mark the Sonoran Desert here, shielding their crops from the intense sun and reducing the amount of water needed.

2 The modern-day version of this can be seen in the Santa Catalina Mountains north of
5   Tucson, where a canopy of elevated solar panels helps to protect rows of squash, tomatoes and onions. Even on a November afternoon, with the temperature climbing into the 80s, the air under the panels stays comfortably cool.

3 Such adaptation is central to the research underway at Biosphere 2, a unique center affiliated with the University of Arizona that's part of a movement aimed at reimagining
10 and remaking agriculture in a warming world. In the Southwest, projects are looking to plants and farming practices that Native Americans have long used as potential solutions to growing worries over future food supplies. At the same time, they are seeking to build energy resilience.

4 Learning from and incorporating Indigenous knowledge is important, believes Greg
15 Barron-Gafford, a professor who studies the intersection of plant biology and environmental and human factors. But instead of relying on tree shade, "we're underneath an energy producer that's not competing for water."

5 On both sides of the Arizona border with Mexico, scientists are planting experimental gardens and pushing the potential of an "agrivoltaic" approach. Thirsty crops such as fruits, nuts and leafy greens — which require elaborate irrigation systems that have pulled vast quantities of water from underground aquifers and the Colorado and other rivers — are nowhere to be found.

6 "We've had 5,000 years of farmers trying out different strategies for dealing with heat, drought and water scarcity," said Gary Nabhan, an ethnobotanist and agrarian activist who focuses on plants and cultures of the Southwest. Collectively, he added, "we need to begin to translate that."

7 Some of the methods at Biosphere 2 — a facility marked by the largest closed ecological system in the world — are being applied in fishing villages on the parched Sonoran coast of Mexico. A multiyear effort there will help ensure water, energy and food sources for some 1,500 members of the Comcaac (or Seri) community.

8 Other researchers are creating a sustainability model for urban settings. The University of Arizona's Desert Laboratory on Tumamoc Hill will break ground next spring on Tumamoc Resilience Gardens, an initiative to be located at the base of a saguaro-studded hill within an 860-acre ecological preserve in the heart of Tucson. It will show how people can feed themselves in a much hotter, drier future.

9 The core of the project's design will be passive rainwater harvesting to support a variety of edible, arid-adapted plants. Some of those will be planted under solar panels, said lab director Benjamin Wilder, while others will benefit from centuries-old strategies such as rock berms and rock piles to increase moisture.

10 Southern Arizona is an epicenter of the movement not just because of the intense environmental pressures that the region faces but because of the presence of the Tohono O'odham Nation southwest of Tucson.

11 The Tohono O'odham have farmed in the Sonoran Desert for several thousand years. Like many Indigenous groups, they now are on the front lines of climate change, with food security a paramount concern. Their expansive reservation, nearly the size of Connecticut, has just a few grocery stores. It is a food desert in a desert where conditions are only getting more extreme.

12 Since the early 1970s, a group of Nation members have run the San Xavier Cooperative

Farm and grown "traditional desert cultivars" in accordance with their ancestral values —
50 particularly respect for land, water and plants.

13 Sterling Johnson, a member of the Tohono O'odham Nation, has worked for the past decade to share that expertise broadly. His partner, Nina Sajovec, directs the Ajo Center for Sustainable Agriculture, a Native American-governed food justice organization that several years ago founded its own seed bank and already has distributed over 10,000 seeds
55 to farmers.

14 "We're all about using what is out there," Sajovec said. Among the center's heirloom varieties: 60-day corn, a fast-maturing desert-adapted vegetable, and the tepary bean, a high-protein legume particularly suited to the climate because of leaves that can fold to withstand direct sunlight during the peak of summer.

60 **15** Johnson captures precipitation during the Arizona monsoon season to sustain crops on his field in the desert lowlands. "It's using the rainwater," he explained, "using the contour lines, using your environment and nature to grow food."

16 This once common dryland farming practice was all but erased by this country's Indian boarding school system, which "ripped" children away from their families and severed
65 the transfer of knowledge, he noted. The increasing interest in Native ways is generally welcome, yet it can feel once again like "Anglo society taking when they need something. We really would like to see these crops and techniques … still used to serve the Native community."

 CD3-06

17 Perhaps even more daunting than the rising temperatures of climate change are the
70 water shortages that many parts of the world will confront. In Tucson, the Santa Cruz River is now dry because of too much diversion and burgeoning demand, according to Brad Lancaster, an expert on rainwater harvesting.

18 "The majority of the water that irrigates landscapes and Tucson and Arizona is not local water" but tapped from the Colorado River, Lancaster said. Unless severe drought
75 conditions reverse and the river level improves, mandatory federal cutbacks mean farmers will lose a significant amount of that critical resource starting next year.

19 "The goal is how can we use rainwater and storm water, passively captured, to be the primary irrigator," said Lancaster, who lives in a local neighborhood that has been transformed through passive water harvesting into an "urban forest," with wild edible

80 plants such as chiltepin pepper and desert hackberry lining the sidewalks.

20 He is planning a similar system at Tumamoc Resilience Gardens, using basins and earthen structures to spread water across the landscape and reduce channelized flows. Nabhan, who also is involved in the site's design, sees it as replicable and, more importantly, scalable.

85 **21** "We hope [planting] these gardens will be the same as planting an apple orchard," Nabhan said, walking around his own creation at his home in Patagonia, a small town about 18 miles north of the Mexico border. The fenced space holds 40 species of agave, three species of sotol, prickly pear and other varieties of cactuses and succulents. "The key concept," he said, "is that we're trying to fit the crops to the environment rather than
90 remaking the environment."

1,089 words

By Samuel Gilbert, Dec. 10, 2021, The Washington Post

Notes

ℓ.8　Biosphere 2「バイオスフィア2」:
アメリカ・アリゾナ州オラクルにある研究施設。世界最大の閉鎖生態系であり、地球科学や生態系、特に近年は気候変動による影響についての研究を主な目的とする。数度の所有権移転を経て、現在(2023年)はアリゾナ大学(The University of Arizona)が所有している。

ℓ.19　agrivoltaic「営農型太陽光発電」:
agriculture と photovoltaics を合わせた造語。農地に太陽光発電設備を設置し、太陽光を農業生産と発電とで共有する取り組みをさす。

ℓ.30　Comcaac (or Seri)「セリ族」:
メキシコ北西部ソノラ地方の海岸に住むアメリカ先住民族の一民族。

ℓ.41　Tohono O'odham「トホノ・オオダム族」:
アメリカ先住民族の一つで、トホノ語で「砂漠の民」を意味する。数千年前からアメリカとメキシコにまたがるソノラ砂漠(Sonoran Desert)で遊牧生活を送ってきた。現在は連邦政府公認の部族で、アリゾナ州とメキシコ北部ソノラ州を主な居住地としている。Tohono O'odham Nation はアリゾナにある先住民居留地の一つ。

ℓ.45　reservation「インディアン居留地」:
先住民族が領有する土地。1830年に白人と先住民族との間に結ばれたインディアン強制移住法により、荒れ地の多いミシシッピ以西の地への移住を虐げられた。

ℓ.63　Indian boarding school「インディアン寄宿学校」:
17世紀半ばから20世紀初頭にかけて行われた、アメリカ先住民の若年層をヨーロッパ系アメリカ文化に同化させるための教育を実施するための施設。多くの施設で、子どもたちは家族から強制的に引き離され、先住民のアイデンティティや文化を放棄することを余儀なくされた。

1. The crops once planted under the trees by Native Americans to avoid the sun and heat are grown under the shade of solar panels in modern times.   [   ]

2. The project at Tumamoc Resilience Gardens involves planting fruits and nuts.   [   ]

3. A group within Tohono O'odham Nation follows their ancestors' approach to agriculture of respecting nature.   [   ]

4. The dryland farming practice inherited by Sterling Johnson has been continuously passed down to Native American children.   [   ]

5. According to Brad Lancaster, most of the irrigation water in Tucson comes from the Colorado River due to the severe drought conditions.   [   ]

Question & **A**nswer | 次の質問に英文で答えましょう。

1. What is the main purpose of the research at Biosphere 2?

_____

2. Why is Santa Cruz River facing water shortages?

_____

3. How has Lancaster's local neighborhood been transformed into an "urban forest"?

_____

Correction & **L**istening | 以下は5箇所の文法上の誤りを含んだ記事の要約文です。誤りを正しく直しましょう。その後、正しい音声を聞いて答えを確認しましょう。

 CD3-07

In the American desert, botanists is growing native plants beneath solar panels. The solar panels get energy to the sun while also providing shade for the plants. Native American learned to cultivate these plants over millennia by attempting various strategies to deal with heat, drought, and water shortages. Elsewhere, projects for efficient use of captured rainwater are taking place, and a Native American food organization has found a seed bank to preserve local species. One of the botanists mentioned that the key concept of their projects is to try to fit the crops to the environmental instead of remaking the environment.

Reflecting on the Whole Article

本章の記事では、温暖化や水不足からやがては食糧難が予測されるこの時代に、かつてネイティブ・アメリカンが行っていた「環境を変えるのではなく、作物を環境に合わせる」農法を再現するプロジェクトについて紹介している。技術や知恵についてだけでなく、根底に流れるネイティブ・アメリカンの信条に触れることで、自然に寄り添って生きる大切さを改めて考えさせられる記事である。

 以下は記事全体の流れと、キーとなる英文です。ペアまたはグループを作り、これらの英文を読んで感じたことをシェアしましょう。その後、各メンバーで分担して次の質問について考え、答えを発表し合いましょう。

Paragraphs **1 − 4**

食料補給とエネルギー供給を同時に〜ネイティブ・アメリカンの知恵から学ぶ〜

..., *"we're underneath an energy producer that's not competing for water."*

(Greg Barron-Gafford)

Q What kind of energy producer is this, and why is it helpful?

Paragraphs **5 − 10**

砂漠で生まれた古来の知恵が応用された農業プロジェクトの紹介

"We've had 5,000 years of farmers trying out different strategies for dealing with heat, drought and water scarcity" (Gary Nabhan)

Q One of the strategies is being applied in the University of Arizona's Desert Laboratory. What kind of an initiative is it?

Paragraphs **11 − 16**

トホノオーダム族が築いた独自の栽培法、背景にある複雑な歴史

Johnson [a member of the Tohono O'odahm Nation] captures precipitation during the Arizona monsoon season to sustain crops on his field in the desert lowlands.

Q Why is this previously widespread farming technique rarely used?

Paragraphs **17 − 21**

深刻さを増す水不足の中で〜雨水利用技術で "urban forest" をつくる試み〜

"We hope [planting] these gardens will be the same as planting an apple orchard"

(Gary Nabhan)

Q Describe how the gardens that Nabhan is discussing are created.

Discussing the Issues

環境の変化に順応して生きるためには何が必要となるだろうか。以下は、本章の記事に寄せられたコメントである。

 Posting Your **C**omment 　次のコメントを参考に、あなた自身の意見を書いてみましょう。

Agnes Lee, *5 hours ago*
Using plants suited to the desert is a great approach in thinly populated areas, but what can we do about major cities in the desert, such as Las Vegas?

ecofan, *3 hours ago*
We have much to learn from Indigenous peoples. We should be interviewing the elders and preserving their knowledge before it dies out.

Jack Harwood, *2 hours ago*
The real problem is that we waste too much water. We need to take responsibility for our own water usage. I heard many people prefer not to eat meat so that they can save water, which is used indirectly to feed the animals. What is your solution?

You, *now*

_____

_____

_____

 Window to Further Research

気候変動による気温の上昇や水不足などの緊急対策が求められるなか、今世界各地で古来の農業システムが注目され、実践されている。さまざまな農法について知見を深めるには以下の文献がおすすめである。

 The Worm Farmer's Handbook: Mid- to Large-Scale Vermicomposting for Farms, Businesses, Municipalities, Schools, and Institutions
by Rhonda Sherman, Chelsea Green Publishing, 2018
『種の起源』で知られる生物学者チャールズ・ダーウィンはミミズ研究でも知られる。ミミズ農法は有機農法のひとつとして今や世界中で実践されている。本著はミミズ農法の計画から実践、実行可能な商業規模の運営などまでのアプローチを分かりやすく説明している。

The One-Straw Revolution: An Introduction to Natural Farming
by Masanobu Fukuoka, New York Review Books Classics, 2009
禅の考えを取り入れた自然界とのバランスに則った持続可能な有機農法は海外でも注目されている。農業の範囲を超えて、廃棄・消費という文明とは異なる哲学的視点を提供している。

Chapter 12

Hidden Network Inside the Forests

The Washington Post

Deforestation is becoming a problem in many parts of Japan, but loggers claim there is no problem because they plant new trees. What do you think?

Vocabulary Sorting

次の語句をカテゴリーに分類しましょう。未知語はペアで意味を確認しましょう。

clear-cut	symbiont	wither	bough
stem	leaf	logging	interdependent
cooperation	replant	harvest	alliance
erosion	root	rip up	invasive

Plant structure	Collaboration	Forestry work	Damaging
·	·	·	·
·	·	·	·
·	·	·	·
·	·	·	·

Words in Context

日本語のヒントを参考に、上の語句から適切な表現を選び、必要な場合は文に合うように形を変えて空欄に記入しましょう。   ◎ CD3-08

Trees in a natural forest develop underground networks, linking together to form an 1. _____ with the help of fungi acting as 2. _____ that connect the

(同盟)   (共生者)

spreading tree 3. _____. Unfortunately, logging companies are 4. _____

(根)   (破壊する)

the large "mother trees" in an area before spraying them with herbicides. They then

5. _____ the area, but the fungi that have lost their connection to the mother trees

(植え直す)

may 6. _____, and the health of the new forest suffers as a result.

(枯れる)

Reading the Article

 CD3-09

With forests in peril, she's on a mission to save 'mother trees'

1 Suzanne Simard walks into the forest with a churchgoer's reverence. The soaring canopies of Douglas firs are her cathedral's ceiling. Shifting branches of cedars, maples and hemlocks filter the sunlight like stained-glass windows. A songbird chorus echoes from the treetops, accompanied by the wind whistling through pine boughs and a woodpecker's
5 steady drumming.

2 But beauty alone is not what makes this place sacred to Simard. In each colossal tree, the University of British Columbia forest ecologist sees a source of oxygen, a filter for water and a home for hundreds of different creatures. Crouching low, Simard pulls a trowel from her pocket and cuts deep into the earth, through layers of moss, duff and debris. "See
10 this?" In her cupped hands, she holds a palmful of soil flecked with thin, white filaments. "Mycorrhizal fungi," she says. "It's joining all these trees together."

3 Through decades of study, Simard and other ecologists have revealed how fungi and trees are linked in vast, subterranean networks through which organisms send messages and swap resources. The findings have helped revolutionize the way the world sees forests,
15 turning static stands of trees into complex societies of interdependent species, where scenes of both fierce competition and startling cooperation play out on a grand scale.

4 Now, Simard is attempting to translate that research into a road map for protecting forests from the demands of logging and the ravages of climate change. In an experiment spanning hundreds of miles, she and her colleagues aim to show the benefits of preserving
20 "mother trees" — giant elders of the forest, which Simard believes play a critical role in maintaining fungal networks, nurturing younger seedlings and safeguarding millions of tons of carbon stored in vegetation and soil.

5 "What it comes down to," she says, "is we have to save our forests, or we're done. ... It comes down to whether we value our environment as something to take from, or
25 something to tend." Simard brushes dirt from her hands, then trudges to the edge of the stand. "Let's go see the clear cut."

⊙ CD3-10

6 On the other side of the road is a 50-acre expanse of tree stumps, shrubs and child-sized Douglas fir saplings. A sign identifies it as part of Simard's Mother Tree Project, one of five experimental plots in the Malcolm Knapp Research Forest, an hour east of
30 Vancouver, Canada.

7 Simard's career began in landscapes like this one. The daughter and granddaughter of tree cutters, her first job was as a forester for a Canadian logging company, flagging the biggest and most valuable trees to be harvested and hauled away. Afterward, the clear-cut site would be sprayed with herbicides — a measure meant to help newly planted
35 commercial seedlings by killing off competitors for sunshine and nutrients. But Simard noticed the replanted landscapes didn't appear as healthy as the forests they had replaced. "It just felt wrong," she says. "I saw the forest as a connected place ... and we were ripping it apart."

8 So she sought out evidence to support her instincts. For her doctoral thesis at Oregon
40 State University, Simard used radioactive carbon as a chemical tracer to show sugars moving between trees of different species connected by the fungal network. When one tree was moved into the shade, making it harder to perform photosynthesis, it received extra carbon from the other plant.

9 Scientists now know that over 90 percent of all terrestrial plants form mycorrhizal
45 partnerships — the legacy of a half-billion-year-old alliance that likely helped plants migrate from the oceans onto land. The fungi provide a foundation for underground food webs. Their lacy architecture retain filter water and prevent erosion by giving structure to the soil.

10 And, crucially, these networks serve as a link in the biological chain that shuttles carbon from the air, into trees, through fungi and then deep into the ground. Studies suggest that as much as 20 percent of the carbon taken up by plants is transferred to their fungal symbionts, allowing the world's mycorrhizal fungi to sequester at least 5 billion tons of carbon dioxide each year. Moreover, Simard's studies have showed that emerging plants fare better when mycorrhizal fungi connect them to mother trees.

CD3-11

11 Despite the revolution in scientists' understanding of this terrain, Simard says forestry hasn't changed much since her early days in the woods. Researchers estimate that more than 90 percent of British Columbia's towering ancient forests have been cut down, and another 94,000 acres of old growth is lost each year. The vast majority of this logging involves clear-cuts or "clear-cuts with reserves," where just a tiny patch of trees is left standing, leaving mycorrhizal fungi to wither without their plant partners.

12 And when trees are removed from a landscape, it unleashes the carbon buried below, studies by Simard and others show. A 2019 report by the Sierra Club found that logged and replanted forests in British Columbia remain net carbon emitters for at least 13 years after being harvested. The province's own data show that forest management generates more than 40 million tons of carbon dioxide each year — equal to the annual emissions from 101 gas-fired power plants. "It's just so crazy," Simard says. "We're ripping up our carbon sinks and using petrol to ship it all over the world. ... We're just making the problem worse."

CD3-12

13 Simard's experiment encompasses nine forest sites scattered across more than 600 miles of British Columbia, each with slightly different environmental circumstances. This creates a "climatic gradient," Simard says, allowing her to test how forests function in varying conditions and predict what might happen as temperatures rise and precipitation dwindles.

14 At every site, Simard partnered with logging companies to conduct five "treatments," or harvesting methods. They visit each plot every year or so, taking several days to document each tree, shrub, moss and mushroom. Planted seedlings get a checkup. Fungi are collected for DNA tests. Leaves, debris and soil are packed away into dozens of brown paper bags; when they get back to the lab, technicians dehydrate the material and calculate how much carbon it contains. The full results of the Mother Tree experiment won't be known until the replanted forests reach maturity, decades from now. But some takeaways are already clear, Simard says.

15 Given the immense amount of carbon stored in ancient, uncut forests, she believes governments should cease all logging there. "It just doesn't make sense," she says. "Any trees that are planted are going to take hundreds, if not thousands, of years to recover those carbon pools. And that's outside the time frame we have to change things."

85 **16** Simard spots a spindly Douglas fir tree, barely a foot high. Its stem is faintly curved — a sign of a tree that has sprouted on its own. Once more, Simard retrieves her trowel and gently works the tree free of the soil, exposing an expansive tangle of roots entwined with barely discernible threads of fungi. "It's a natural," she confirms. Unlike pampered, nursery-grown trees, the fir had to develop an "exploratory" root system to get the nutrients
90 it needed.

17 Now, whatever threats loom ahead of the forest — drought, invasive plants, nutrient shortages — the tree's ample roots and mycorrhizal partners will help it access what it needs to survive. Gently, she nestles the sapling back into the earth, then empties her water bottle into the parched ground. "Good luck," she says. "Good luck little tree."

1,220 words

By Sarah Kaplan, Dec. 27, 2022, *The Washington Post*

Notes

ℓ.7 the University of British Columbia (UBC)「ブリティッシュ・コロンビア大学」:
カナダのブリティッシュ・コロンビア州にある、北米を代表する名門大学。さまざまな分野での高レベルの教育・研究には定評があり、世界大学ランキングでは常に上位に入る。また森と海に囲まれた立地もあり、森林科学や海洋学などの自然科学分野の研究でも定評がある。

ℓ.28 Mother Tree Project「マザーツリー・プロジェクト」:
2015年にシマードらが中心となり発足された大規模なプロジェクト。森林の地下におけるネットワーク、特にベイマツのマザーツリーと苗木間の地中でのつながりが伐採や再生処理後の森林の回復力にどのような影響を与えるかを主に研究している。

ℓ.29 Malcolm Knapp Research Forest「マルコム・ナップ研究林」:
ブリティッシュ・コロンビア州メープル・リッジのコースト山脈に位置する森林。面積は約5,157ヘクタール。1800年代から大規模な伐採が行われていたが、1929年の大恐慌後に林業が衰退し、その後一帯はUBCの管理下に置かれ、前述のマザーツリー・プロジェクトをはじめ、さまざまな森林研究が実施されている。名称はこの森林の拡充にも尽力し、その後の森林研究に多大な影響を与えたUBCのマルコム・ナップ教授に因む。トレッキングやキャンプ地としても人気がある。

ℓ.39 Oregon State University「オレゴン州立大学」:
アメリカ・オレゴン州に本拠を置く研究型総合大学。7,000エーカー（東京ドーム約608個分）に及ぶ演習林があり、森林研究は世界トップクラスの水準を誇る。

ℓ.40 chemical tracer「科学トレーサ」:
液体や特定の物質の移動や化学反応などを追跡するために使われるもの。この実験では炭素ガスを植物に注入し、その植物が地下で近くの木々に炭素を送っているかどうかを調べた。

True or **F**alse | 英文を読んで、本文と合致する場合は T を、合致しない場合は F を記入し
ましょう。

1. When working as a forester, Simard marked the biggest trees that were withering and needed to be carried away. [   ]

2. It is said that almost all the plants on Earth form mycorrhizal partenerships. [   ]

3. Logging in British Columbia has recently been restricted to protect the forests. [   ]

4. The "treatments" Simard and logging companies do include checkups of plants, collecting fungi for DNA tests, and calculating the amount of carbon within the plants. [   ]

5. The results of Simard's Mother Tree experiment will be revealed soon. [   ]

Question & **A**nswer | 次の質問に英文で答えましょう。

1. What did Simard and other ecologists find out about the relation between fungi and trees?

_____

2. What did Simard notice when she was working for the logging company?

_____

3. What did the Sierra Club find out in the 2019 report?

_____

Correction & **L**istening | 以下は5箇所の文法上の誤りを含んだ記事の要約文です。誤りを正しく直しましょう。その後、正しい音声を聞いて答えを確認しましょう。

🔘 CD3-13

   Suzanne Simard is an ecologist which is working on preserve "mother trees," which are the giant elders of the forest. Simard has discovered these trees are essential of maintain fungal networks among variety species that send messages and swap resources, such as sugar and carbon. Studies also show that these networks play a crucial role in sequestering large amounts of carbon dioxide. In spite of these remarkable finding, forestry has changed little in recent decades. Simard thinks the government should cease all logging and insists that we have to change the way we do forest work.

Reflecting on the Whole Article

植物同士が必要な養分を補い合うネットワークを形成しているという驚くべき事実を明らかにしたシマード博士。森の情景描写から始まり、科学的な研究とその結果、そこから浮かび上がる世界の課題を述べ、また森の描写に戻る本記事の展開には読者をテーマに惹きつける巧みさがある。

 以下は記事全体の流れと、キーとなる英文です。ペアまたはグループを作り、これらの英文を読んで感じたことをシェアしましょう。その後、各メンバーで分担して次の質問について考え、答えを発表し合いましょう。

Paragraphs 1 — 5

森林と共にあるシマード博士の半生、彼女の長年の研究「マザーツリー保護プロジェクト」の紹介

Now, Simard is attempting to translate that research into a road map for protecting forests from the demands of logging and the ravages of climate change.

Q Explain what Simard is aiming to do in her research.

Paragraphs 6 — 10

シマード博士の研究の軌跡 ～材木会社勤務時代に感じた違和感から植物間ネットワークの解明まで～

"I saw the forest as a connected place … and we were ripping it apart."

(Suzanne Simard)

Q What is one example that shows the forest as a connected place?

Paragraphs 11 — 12

ブリティッシュ・コロンビアの森林伐採とそれに伴うCO_2排出

Despite the revolution in scientists' understanding of this terrain, Simard says forestry hasn't changed much since her early days in the woods.

Q What is forestry's methodology in British Columbia, Canada, and why is it wrong-headed?

Paragraphs 13 — 17

「マザーツリー保護プロジェクト」の現状と今後の兆し、シマード博士の森に対する想い

The full results of the Mother Tree experiment won't be known until the replanted forests reach maturity, decades from now. But some takeaways are already clear, Simard says.

Q What clear conclusion did Simard draw from her research?

Discussing the Issues

植物が人間と同じようにコミュニケーションをとり助け合って生きているということを知りどう感じた
だろうか。林業や森林伐採などの問題も含めて自分の意見を述べてみよう。以下は、本章の記事に
寄せられたコメントである。

 Posting Your **C**omment 　　次のコメントを参考に、あなた自身の意見を書いてみましょう。

Matt, *12 hours ago*
Now that we know trees and plants form a network of their own, it seems so cruel to
tear some parts off by logging or deforestation.

Suzuki, *4 hours ago*
Some say that if you cut down trees, you can just replant them somewhere else, but
it takes a tremendous amount of time to get a forest back to the same condition as
before. So, we should stop logging.

Tree hugger, *3 hours ago*
With eight billion people living in the world, we need some way to provide the resources
we need, and wood is still important for housing. We cannot stop all logging. The
question is, how to find a balance between logging and sustaining the forests.

You, *now*

 Window to Further Research

環境破壊やそれに起因する自然災害に歯止めがかからない今、我々は自然と
どのように向き合い行動していくべきであろうか。まずは森を歩き、森のささ
やく声に耳を傾けてみよう。以下はその手引書である。

 *The Hidden Life of Trees: What They Feel, How They Communicate*
by Peter Wohlleben, William Collins, 2017
ドイツの森林管理官だった著者は、樹木は家族をもち、
栄養を分かち合い、コミュニケーションをとり、危険が
迫れば警告し合うという。そのような生態から森林はひ
とつのソーシャルネットワークであると提唱する。

 Silent Spring
by Rachel Carson, Penguin Modern Classics, 2000
DDTや殺虫剤、農薬などの化学物質の乱用により、動植
物の静まり返る「沈黙の春」を警告した世界初の環境問
題の告発本。1962年に出版されて、現在も環境問題のバ
イブルとして広く読まれている。臨場感に溢れ、短めで読
みやすいので、ぜひ洋書で読んで欲しい一冊である。

Chapter 13

The True Cost of Fast Fashion

The Guardian

Whose responsibility is it to make sure that clothes are produced ethically: the clothing companies, governments, or consumers?

Vocabulary Sorting

次の語句をカテゴリーに分類しましょう。未知語はペアで意味を確認しましょう。

oversized	wage	talk about being natural	textile factory
garment	hoodie	attach labels	social media promotion
greenwashing	launch	offshore production	rock-bottom price
gross	crop top	disposable income	customer expectation

Clothing	Economic term	Supply chain	Marketing strategy
•	•	•	•
•	•	•	•
•	•	•	•
•	•	•	•

Words in Context

日本語のヒントを参考に、上の語句から適切な表現を選び、必要な場合は文に合うように形を変えて空欄に記入しましょう。　　CD3-14

If you want to buy a **1.** _____ that has been made ethically, you should not
                              衣服

buy it at a **2.** _____. The very cheap clothes are made by paying
                                        最安値

low **3.** _____ to people working in the **4.** _____ in developing
            賃金   織物工場

countries. Companies try to advertise their green status through various channels such as

5. _____, boasting that their products are sustainably made,
                        SNS の宣伝

which is often questionable or quite different from the reality. Giving a wrong impression to

the consumer in this way is known as **6.** _____.
                                                          見せかけの環境広報活動

Reading the Article

 CD3-15

The truth about fast fashion: can you tell how ethical your clothing is by its price?

1 What is the true cost of a Zara hoodie? In April 2019, David Hachfeld of the Swiss NGO Public Eye, along with a team of researchers and the Clean Clothes Campaign, attempted to find out. They chose to analyse a black, oversized top from Zara's flagship Join Life sustainability line, which was printed with lyrics made famous by Aretha Franklin:

5 "R-E-S-P-E-C-T: find out what it means to me." It was an apt choice, because the idea was to work out whether any respect had been paid to the workers involved in the garment's production, and how much of the hoodie's average retail price, €26.66 (£22.70), went into their pockets.

2 Their research suggested that the biggest chunk of the hoodie's retail price — an estimated

10 €10.26 — went back into Zara, to cover retail space and staff wages. The next biggest slice,

after VAT at €4.44, was profit for Inditex/Zara, at €4.20. Their research suggested that the textile factory in Izmir received just €1.53 for cutting the material, sewing, packing and attaching the labels, with €1.10 of that being paid to the garment workers for the 30-minute job of putting the hoodie together. The report concluded that workers could not have received anything like a living wage, which the Clean Clothes Campaign defined, at the time the report was released, as a gross hourly wage of €6.19.

3 When the research was covered by the media at the time, Zara said the report was "based on erroneous premises and inaccurate reporting." But at the time and when I contacted Zara for this article, the company declined to set out in greater detail where the research was inaccurate.

4 What is clear is that trying to find out the true production cost of a garment is a tortuous and potentially fruitless process — even when assessing a major high street retailer's flagship "sustainability" line. Hachfeld points out that Zara is by no means uniquely opaque. Vanishingly few retailers guarantee living wages across their vast, complex supply chains. According to the not-for-profit group Fashion Revolution, only two of the world's 250 largest fashion brands (OVS and Patagonia) disclose how many of their workers are paid a living wage — despite the kind of resources that make billionaires of founders.

CD3-16

5 Throughout fashion, the numbers just don't add up. High-street clothing has been getting cheaper and cheaper for decades. A major reason why, according to Gordon Renouf, the CEO of the fashion ethics comparison app Good on You, is that so many western brands have "moved from onshore production 40 years ago to larger offshore production." Often, the countries they have chosen have "much lower wage costs, weaker labour movements and laxer environmental regulations." Of course, we know all this, but we have also become accustomed to reaping the benefits. Our perception of what clothing should cost — and how much of it we need — has shifted.

6 In 1970, for example, the average British household spent 7% of its annual income on clothing. This had fallen to 5.9% by 2020. Even though we are spending less proportionally, we tend to own more clothes. According to the UN, the average consumer buys 60% more pieces of clothing — with half the lifespan — than they did 15 years ago. Meanwhile, fashion is getting cheaper: super-fast brands such as Shein (which sells tie-dye crop tops for £1.49) and Alibaba (vest tops for $2.20), have boomed online, making high-street brands look slow-moving and expensive by comparison.

7 But the correlation between price and ethics is knotty, to say the least. On the high street, many who proudly opt out of shopping at Primark or Boohoo for ethical reasons
45 may be unaware that most reassuringly mid-priced brands don't guarantee workers living wages or produce clothing without using environmentally harmful materials. A garment's price is often more about aspiration and customer expectation than the cost of production. Hachfeld points out that the Zara hoodie was priced higher in Switzerland (CHF 45.90; €39.57), where Zara is positioned as a mid-range brand, than in Spain (€25.95), where it
50 is perceived as more mainstream and affordable.

8 The sustainable-fashion writer Aja Barber uses the phrase "exploitation prices" to refer to very cheap clothes. "Any time a dress is under £50, you really need to break down the labour on it," she says. "Think about what you get paid hourly — think, could a person make this dress in three hours?" In her view, fast fashion is propped up not by those with
55 very low disposable incomes, but by middle-class overconsumption.

9 The only way to tell if a garment has been ethically produced is by combing through the details on the manufacturer's website (although many brands give little or no information.) Even among brands that have launched with sustainability, greenwashing is rife. Renouf warns against those that talk vaguely about being "natural" and "fair," or bang on about
60 recycled packaging, without giving details about, say, the materials they use or whether they engage with unions in their factories.

10 For the fashion retailer Sam Mabley, the idea that fashion can be ethical only if it is expensive is a myth. Mabley runs a sustainable fashion store in Bristol; he thought it was a shame that he was selling so many ethical T-shirts at around the £30 price point. Usually,
65 he says, such T-shirts are created in small batches, by "cool indie brands who do printed designs — a lot of the work is in the design." He decided to invert that business model, ramping up the scale in order to get bigger discounts from suppliers and creating plain, organic cotton, ethically produced Ts in black and white for £7.99. With just a month of social media promotion, he secured 4,000 orders.

70 **11** Jenny Hulme, the head of buying at the sustainable fashion mainstay People Tree, believes ethical production is necessary and possible in every part of the market. "If you order in big volumes, it does reduce price — if a company really wants to improve, it can," she says. The reality of high-street clothes shopping is still very far from this ideal, because the business models that have enabled clothing to get this cheap rely on inexpensive,

75 environmentally damaging fabrics and very low wages.

12 Voting with your wallet will only go so far, however, and won't be possible for many people who are struggling, as the number of people in poverty in the UK soars to 15 million. Questioning the magical thinking of rock-bottom prices is not about blaming the consumer. Instead, you could write to MPs and CEOs and demand that they do something 80 about living wages and the environmental cost of fashion. The responsibility lies with brands, and with the government, which should be held to account for a broken system.

1,114 words

By Hannah Marriott, Jul. 29, 2021, *The Guardian*

Notes

ℓ.2 Public Eye「パブリック・アイ」:
スイスに本部を置く人権NGO団体で、主に労働環境において貧困国の人権と環境を尊重するように働きかけを行っている。1968年設立。なお、2021年11月に同団体は本文に登場するSheinの中国にある生産拠点を調査し、現地の労働法に反する危険な労働環境での生産体制を告発した。

ℓ.2 Clean Clothes Campaign(CCC)「クリーン・クローズ・キャンペーン」:
1989年に設立された国際NGOで、衣料業界における労働条件の改善と労働者のエンパワーメントを主な目的とする。現在は日本を含む45カ国で230以上の支部がある。

ℓ.4 Aretha Franklin: "R-E-S-P-E-C-T: find out what it means to me":
Respectは'クイーン・オブ・ソウル'アレサ・フランクリンの代表曲。元々は60年代を代表する男性ソウル歌手オーティス・レディングの自作曲で、つれない自身の妻に対し「俺をもっと尊重(リスペクト)してくれよ」と歌う夫の悲哀に満ちた楽曲だが、アレサはこれを女性の権利を主張する歌にアレンジし、オリジナルを凌駕するヒット作となった。R-E-S-P-E-C-Tとスペルアウトし、find out what it means to me(それが私にとってどんな意味なのか気付いて)と叫ぶパートはオリジナルにはなく、アレサが新たに加えたもの。

ℓ.25 Fashion Revolution「ファッション・レボリューション」:
環境保護とファッション業界に携わる人々の保護を目的とする活動家団体。2013年にバングラデッシュで起きた有名アパレルの生産拠点ビルの崩壊事故を受けて設立された。事故現場となったラナプラザビルは以前から崩壊の危険性が指摘されていたにもかかわらず、利益を優先したオーナーがビル内の下請け工場で働く労働者を脅迫、徹夜で働かせるなどした結果、死者約1,130人、行方不明者約500人、負傷者2,500人以上にのぼる犠牲者を出す大惨事となった。

ℓ.44 Primark「プライマーク」:
アイルランド発のファストファッションブランド。かつて同社の商品タグに、生産者が書き込んだとみられる劣悪な労働環境を告発するメッセージが発見され話題になった。

ℓ.44 Boohoo「ブーフー」:
イギリス発のカジュアルファッションブランド。

ℓ.70 People Tree「ピープルツリー」:
イギリス発のフェアトレード専門ブランド。

True or **F**alse 　英文を読んで、本文と合致する場合は T を、合致しない場合は F を記入しましょう。

1. When the media reported the research, Zara contested the accuracy of the results. [　　]

2. The process of finding out the true production cost of a garment is troublesome and often ends up being unsuccessful. [　　]

3. Between 1970 and 2020, British consumers spent less on clothes but bought more pieces, which indicates that fashion is getting cheaper. [　　]

4. Aja Barber thinks that the fast-fashion industry is supported by low-wage workers. [　　]

5. According to Renouf, it is safe to buy clothes from brands launched as sustainable because the brands stress the "natural" and "fair" quality of the items. [　　]

Question & **A**nswer 　次の質問に英文で答えましょう。

1. What was the purpose of finding out the true cost of a Zara hoodie?

_____

2. What do many shoppers not know about mid-priced brands?

_____

3. What does the article suggest readers do to promote ethical production?

_____

Correction & **L**istening 　以下は 5 箇所の文法上の誤りを含んだ記事の要約文です。誤りを正しく直しましょう。その後、正しい音声を聞いて答えを確認しましょう。

 CD3-19

An NGO group and a team of researchers conducted research to find out the true cost of fashion, which showed the difficulty of knowing what ethical a company is in reality. We take advantage to the low prices that the clothes are sold at, not considering that the reason they are cheap is that the textile workers are paid very few. Also, we may try to buy ethically by paying attention to labels that say, as example, that the clothing is "natural" or "fair," without providing any evidence. We had better be carefully, as many companies are guilty of greenwashing.

Reflecting on the Whole Article

ファッション業界の裏に潜む深刻な環境汚染や労働者搾取の問題は既知の事実であるが、自然や人に優しいと謳うサステナブルブランドや商品にも同様の問題が根強くあることを本記事は明らかにしている。特に近年人気のファストファッションの価格がなぜ抑えられるのか、その製造工程とコストを客観的に示し、この業界がさまざまな犠牲の上に成り立っていることを、リアリティーを持って伝えている。

 以下は記事全体の流れと、キーとなる英文です。ペアまたはグループを作り、これらの英文を読んで感じたことをシェアしましょう。その後、各メンバーで分担して次の質問について考え、答えを発表し合いましょう。

Paragraphs **1 – 4**

Zaraの「サステナビリティ」の真価を問う──ファッション業界の不透明な製造コスト

What is the true cost of a Zara hoodie?

Q According to David Hachfeld and the research team, how does the cost of a Zara hoodie break down and how much of that money gets paid to the garment workers?

Paragraphs **5 – 6**

ファッションの低価格化とその裏に潜む「搾取の構造」

High-street clothing has been getting cheaper and cheaper for decades.

Q What is a key reason for the decline in prices?

Paragraphs **7 – 10**

価格とエシカルの関係性──「高価＝エシカル」の誤った社会通念

But the correlation between price and ethics is knotty, to say the least.

Q What does a garment's price usually reflect, and how can a customer be sure that a garment is ethical?

Paragraphs **11 – 12**

エシカルへの道のりは長い──企業、政府の説明責任がカギ

The responsibility lies with brands, and with the government, which should be held to account for a broken system.

Q Explain the "broken system."

Discussing the Issues

エシカルファッションへの注目が高まるものの、ファッション業界が抱える環境や人権に対する課題は山積みである。以下は本章の記事に寄せられたコメントである。

次のコメントを参考に、あなた自身の意見を書いてみましょう。

Mai, *8 hours ago*

Wow, I didn't know about the reality of the fashion industry at all! Considering the fact that 92 million tons of clothes end up in landfill annually, consumers, as well as the companies and governments, have to think how to solve this broken system.

Cinnamon, *5 hours ago*

I don't mind paying more than the actual retail price for my clothes, but it's difficult to pay the true ethical price for every item. What's a good compromise?

Commonsense, *3 hours ago*

Garment factories are said to be sweatshops where the workers, who may even be children, work in unsafe conditions. We must think carefully whether we are making the right choice before buying clothes.

You, *now*

_____

_____

_____

Window to Further Research

ファストファッションの現状を知り、消費者として私たちができることは何であろうか。今こそサステナビリティファッションにおける考察と行動が求められているのではないだろうか。以下はそのための推薦書である。

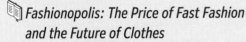

Fashionopolis: The Price of Fast Fashion and the Future of Clothes

by Dana Thomas, Apollo, 2019

世界の劣悪な労働環境、ファッション業界における生産チェーンの複雑な構造、環境問題などについて実例とともに解明。また大手企業による環境問題と人権問題への具体的な取り組み例を紹介している。それは私たちがどのブランドを選択するかという判断基準にもなる。

Loved Clothes Last

by Orsola de Castro, Penguin Life, 2021

丁寧なケアと仕立て直しなどにより、お気に入りの服をより長持ちさせることができるのは喜びである。それはまた人権や労働問題、二酸化炭素削減などの環境対策にもつながる。持続可能なライフスタイルを実現するためのさまざまな具体案を提唱。

Basic Information

創立　　1888年
形態　　月刊誌
本社　　アメリカ合衆国ワシントンD.C.
ロゴについて
　「イエローボーダー」と呼ばれる長方形
　の枠は1910年に表紙を刷新した際に
　黄色い枠が施されたことに由来する。

1888年に地理学の普及を目的に33人の学者らによって設立されたナショナルジオグラフィック協会（National Geographic Society）の協会誌として、同年9月に創刊された。テキスト中心の雑誌から、現在のようなグラフィック中心の内容に切り替わったのは1900年代初頭で、以後は質の高い写真を活かした記事が同誌の特徴として定着する。有名なスクープとして、古代インカ帝国の遺跡マチュピチュの発見や、沈没したタイタニック号の海底での発見などがある。

出版と並行して、協会は映像分野にも進出した。1963年に番組制作会社を設立、その後1997年にナショナルジオグラフィック・チャンネルがスタート。以降、美しい自然の映像や歴史に関する良質なドキュメンタリーで多くの視聴者を獲得する。

現在はウォルト・ディズニー・カンパニーの傘下にある。2023年、同誌は専属ライターを全員解雇し、記事制作をすべて外注する方針を固めた。さらに2024年以降はニューススタンドでの販売を停止すると発表した。

ナショジオ史上、最も有名な写真
「アフガンの少女」

ソ連のアフガン侵攻後の1984年、フォトジャーナリストのスティーブ・マッカリーはパキスタンのペシャワール近郊の難民キャンプで一人の少女を撮影した。赤いスカーフ姿でカメラに厳しい眼差しを向けるその姿は1985年6月号の表紙となり、中東の政情不安や難民のおかれる状況を象徴するものとして、大きな反響を呼んだ。

撮影当時、マッカリーは少女の身元を確認していなかったため、2002年にマッカリーら同誌のチームは彼女を探すために再びアフガニスタンに向かった。捜索は難航を極めたが、ようやくシャーバート・グーラーという女性が当人であることを探し当て、同年2月号で再び表紙を飾った（上記写真）。彼女はこの時まで自分の写真が有名になっていることを全く知らなかった。2021年にタリバンがアフガンを制圧すると、グーラーのような知名度のある女性は脅迫の対象となった。彼女は自らの要請で同年11月にイタリアに亡命した。

INNOVATE

Chapter 14 Should A.I. Contend for Art Prizes?

The New York Times

Moving from paintings to photographs, and black-and-white images to computer graphics, art has always adapted to new technologies. With each new development, we can still say, "This is art." What makes something "art"?

V Vocabulary Sorting

次の語句をカテゴリーに分類しましょう。未知語はペアで意味を確認しましょう。

plagiarism	borderline magic	lump of clay	deceive
fierce	sculpture	photorealistic	recoil
hyper-realistic	backlash	canvas	abstract
graphic	demonically inspired	cheat	

Art form / Material	Art description	Strong reaction	Falsehood
·	·	·	·
·	·	·	·
·	·	·	·
·	·	·	·

W Words in Context

日本語のヒントを参考に、上の語句から適切な表現を選び、必要な場合は文に合うように形を変えて空欄に記入しましょう。　　　○ CD3-20

The use of technology in the art field has been remarkable in recent years, with many A.I.-generated **1.** _____ pieces being presented. Even **2.** _____
超写実的な 彫刻
are designed using 3D printing technology. While some people praise the beauty and high precision of these works, the practice of creating A.I.-generated art has also led to a **3.** _____ **4.** _____. Critics say that the artists have committed
激烈な 反発
5. _____ due to A.I. copying from the internet. This issue is now the subject of
盗作
much debate.

Reading the Article

 CD3-21

An A.I.-generated picture won an art prize. Artists aren't happy.

1 This year, the Colorado State Fair's annual art competition gave out prizes in all the usual categories: painting, quilting, sculpture. But one entrant, Jason M. Allen of Pueblo West, Colo., didn't make his entry with a brush or a lump of clay. He created it with Midjourney, an artificial intelligence program that turns lines of text into hyper-realistic
5 graphics.

2 Mr. Allen's work, "Théâtre D'opéra Spatial," took home the blue ribbon in the fair's contest for emerging digital artists — making it one of the first A.I.-generated pieces to win such a prize, and setting off a fierce backlash from artists who accused him of, essentially, cheating.

10 **3** Reached by phone on Wednesday, Mr. Allen defended his work. He said that he had

made clear that his work — which was submitted under the name "Jason M. Allen via Midjourney" — was created using A.I., and that he hadn't deceived anyone about its origins. "I'm not going to apologize for it," he said. "I won, and I didn't break any rules."

⊙ CD3-22

4 A.I.-generated art has been around for years. But tools released this year — with names like DALL-E 2, Midjourney and Stable Diffusion — have made it possible for rank amateurs to create complex, abstract or photorealistic works simply by typing a few words into a text box.

5 These apps have made many human artists understandably nervous about their own futures — why would anyone pay for art, they wonder, when they could generate it themselves? They have also generated fierce debates about the ethics of A.I.-generated art, and opposition from people who claim that these apps are essentially a high-tech form of plagiarism.

6 Mr. Allen, 39, began experimenting with A.I.-generated art this year. He runs a studio, Incarnate Games, which makes tabletop games, and he was curious how the new breed of A.I. image generators would compare with the human artists whose works he commissioned.

7 This summer, he got invited to a Discord chat server where people were testing Midjourney, which uses a complex process known as "diffusion" to turn text into custom images. Users type a series of words in a message to Midjourney; the bot spits back an image seconds later.

8 Mr. Allen became obsessed, creating hundreds of images and marveling at how realistic they were. No matter what he typed, Midjourney seemed capable of making it. "I couldn't believe what I was seeing," he said. "I felt like it was demonically inspired — like some otherworldly force was involved."

9 Eventually, Mr. Allen got the idea to submit one of his Midjourney creations to the Colorado State Fair, which had a division for "digital art/digitally manipulated photography." He had a local shop print the image on canvas and submitted it to the judges. "The fair was coming up," he said, "and I thought: How wonderful would it be to demonstrate to people how great this art is?"

⊙ CD3-23

10 Several weeks later, while walking the fairground in Pueblo, Mr. Allen saw a blue ribbon hanging next to his piece. He had won the division, along with a $300 prize. "I couldn't believe it," he said. "I felt like: this is exactly what I set out to accomplish." (Mr. Allen declined to share the exact text prompt he had submitted to Midjourney to create "Théâtre D'opéra Spatial." But he said the French translation — "Space Opera Theater" — provided a clue.)

11 After his win, Mr. Allen posted a photo of his prize work to the Midjourney Discord chat. It made its way to Twitter, where it sparked a furious backlash. "We're watching the death of artistry unfold right before our eyes," one Twitter user wrote. "This is so gross," another wrote. "I can see how A.I. art can be beneficial, but claiming you're an artist by generating one? Absolutely not."

12 Some artists defended Mr. Allen, saying that using A.I. to create a piece was no different from using Photoshop or other digital image-manipulation tools, and that human creativity is still required to come up with the right prompts to generate an award-winning piece.

13 Olga Robak, a spokeswoman for the Colorado Department of Agriculture, which oversees the state fair, said Mr. Allen had adequately disclosed Midjourney's involvement when submitting his piece; the category's rules allow any "artistic practice that uses digital technology as part of the creative or presentation process." The two category judges did not know that Midjourney was an A.I. program, she said, but both subsequently told her that they would have awarded Mr. Allen the top prize even if they had.

CD3-24

14 Controversy over new art-making technologies is nothing new. Many painters recoiled at the invention of the camera, which they saw as a debasement of human artistry. (Charles Baudelaire, the 19th-century French poet and art critic, called photography "art's most mortal enemy.") In the 20th century, digital editing tools and computer-assisted design programs were similarly dismissed by purists for requiring too little skill of their human collaborators.

15 What makes the new breed of A.I. tools different, some critics believe, is not just that they're capable of producing beautiful works of art with minimal effort. It's how they work. Apps like DALL-E 2 and Midjourney are built by scraping millions of images from the open web, then teaching algorithms to recognize patterns and relationships in those images and generate new ones in the same style. That means that artists who upload their works to the internet may be unwittingly helping to train their algorithmic competitors. "What makes this AI different is that it's explicitly trained on current working artists," RJ Palmer, a digital artist, tweeted last month. "This thing wants our jobs, its actively anti-artist."

16 Even some who are impressed by A.I.-generated art have concerns about how it's being made. Andy Baio, a technologist and writer, wrote in a recent essay that DALL-E 2, perhaps
75 the buzziest A.I. image generator on the market, was "borderline magic in what it's capable of conjuring, but raises so many ethical questions, it's hard to keep track of them all."

17 Mr. Allen, the blue-ribbon winner, said he empathized with artists who were scared that A.I. tools would put them out of work. But he said their anger should be directed not at individuals who use DALL-E 2 or Midjourney to make art but at companies that choose
80 to replace human artists with A.I. tools. "It shouldn't be an indictment of the technology itself," he said. "The ethics isn't in the technology. It's in the people." And he urged artists to overcome their objections to A.I., even if only as a coping strategy. "This isn't going to stop," Mr. Allen said. "Art is dead, dude. It's over. A.I. won. Humans lost."

1,095 words

By Kevin Roose, Sept. 2, 2022, *The New York Times*

Notes

ℓ.1 the Colorado State Fair「コロラドステートフェア」:
毎年8月にアメリカ・コロラド州プエブロで開催されるイベント。さまざまな催しが行われ、美術コンテストもその一つ。現在は、コロラド州農業局(Colorado Department of Agriculture)の一部門として当局が管轄している。

ℓ.4 Midjourney「ミッドジャーニー」:
AIによる画像生成プログラムの一つ。ユーザーはまずチャットアプリDiscordをインストールし、ここにテキストメッセージを送信すると、その内容から画像が自動生成される。なお、このMidjourneyと後述するStable Diffusionは既存のアーティストやクリエイターの権利を侵害する作品を作成したとして、2023年に開発会社を相手取った集団訴訟がアメリカで提起されている。

ℓ.6 blue ribbon「ブルーリボン」:
映画やアート作品に送られる最高の賞をさす。元々はイギリスの最高勲章である「ガーター勲章」のリボンが青であったことからブルーリボンと呼ばれ、その後いろいろな分野にもこの名称が用いられるようになった。

ℓ.15 DALL-E 2「ダリ ツー」:
ChatGPTの開発元でもあるOpenAI社が2022年に発表した画像生成AIプログラム。

ℓ.15 Stable Diffusion「ステーブルディフュージョン」:
2022年に発表された画像生成AIプログラムで、ミュンヘン大学の研究チームがStability AI社などと共同開発した。コードが一般公開されていて、無料で利用できるのが特徴(2023年現在)。

ℓ.60 Charles Baudelaire「シャルル・ボードレール(1821-1867)」:
19世紀のフランスの詩人・評論家。象徴主義の創始者として知られ、代表作に『悪の華』『パリの憂鬱』などがある。現実を忠実に再現する写実主義や写真技術は芸術ではないと批判した。

$\mathbf{T}^{rue\,or}_{\mathbf{F}alse}$ | 英文を読んで、本文と合致する場合は T を、合致しない場合は F を記入しましょう。

1. Mr. Allen regrets submitting the piece to the competition and winning first prize. [   ]

2. Mr. Allen won the division, but declined to accept the $300 prize money.   [   ]

3. The judges might not have given a blue ribbon to Mr. Allen's work if they had known it was created by an A.I. tool.   [   ]

4. In the 20th century, purists rejected digital editing tools and computer-aided design programs because they were thought to degrade the human capacity to think.   [   ]

5. Mr. Allen thinks companies are to blame for cutting jobs for artists, not the people using A.I. tools.   [   ]

$\mathbf{Q}^{uestion\,\&}_{\mathbf{A}nswer}$ | 次の質問に英文で答えましょう。

1. Why are some recently released art-generating apps making artists nervous?

_____

2. What arguments did Mr. Allen's defenders make about his use of A.I.?

_____

3. According to some critics, what is the critical difference between A.I. art tools and the other art-making technologies?

_____

$\mathbf{C}^{orrection\,\&}_{\mathbf{L}istening}$ | 以下は 5 箇所の文法上の誤りを含んだ記事の要約文です。誤りを正しく直しましょう。その後、正しい音声を聞いて答えを確認しましょう。

CD3-25

The awarding of a prize to an A.I.-inspired artwork created by Jason M. Allen has set up a backlash. Since A.I. gets its inspiration from millions of images from the open web, some people saying it was a form of plagiarize. Other support Mr. Allen on the grounds that the latest technology has often been used in art, but human creativity is still required to make prize-winning works. Mr. Allen himself refuses to apologize, insisting that he didn't break some rules and that the ethics lie not in the technology but in the people.

Reflecting on the Whole Article

本章の記事は、人々のAIアートに対する賛否両論が臨場感を持って繰り広げられている。AIツールを使って生成された絵画が優れた評価を受けたことから、創作における倫理的・権利的問題と、今後芸術の定義そのものがテクノロジーの進化によって変わる可能性が浮き彫りにされた。この問題は芸術だけに限らず、さまざまな業界でも同時多発的に起こっていることといえる。

 以下は記事全体の流れと、キーとなる英文です。ペアまたはグループを作り、これらの英文を読んで感じたことをシェアしましょう。その後、各メンバーで分担して次の質問について考え、答えを発表し合いましょう。

Paragraphs 1 − 3

AIによる絵画が優秀賞に——広がる波紋

"I'm not going to apologize for it," he said. "I won, and I didn't break any rules."
(Jason M. Allen)

Q Why did Mr. Allen say he won't apologize?

_____

Paragraphs 4 − 9

AIアートをめぐる現状とアレン氏が出展に至った経緯

"I felt like it was demonically inspired — like some otherworldly force was involved." (Jason M. Allen)

Q Why does Mr. Allen feel this way about the A.I.-generated art?

Paragraphs 10 − 13

アレン氏の受賞、AIアートをめぐって巻き起こる議論

"We're watching the death of artistry unfold right before our eyes" (Twitter user)

Q Explain what this Twitter user intends to say.

_____

Paragraphs 14 − 17

アートVSテクノロジーの歴史、AIアートに対するアレン氏の見解

"Art is dead, dude. It's over. A.I. won. Humans lost." (Jason M. Allen)

Q What do you think Mr. Allen means by this?

_____

Discussing the Issues

日々進化するアートテクノロジーによって芸術分野は今後どのように変化していくのだろうか。以下は、本章の記事に寄せられたコメントである。

P osting Your C omment　次のコメントを参考に、あなた自身の意見を書いてみましょう。

Angie, *7 hours ago*
This A.I. art reminds me of the many ways art has been faked through the ages; whether it is a fake Picasso or a fake antique, we have always had experts to test for fakes. Some think "faking" itself is an art. Should A.I. art be classified as "fake"?

TEDDY, *2 hours ago*
I think artists will still be able to earn a living in the future. Customers may even pay more for the privilege and certainty of owning a one-of-a-kind piece of art. But meanwhile, we will now need the ability to determine whether the art is made by A.I. or humans.

You, *now*

_____

_____

_____

Window to Further Research

AIアートは「アート」として定義されるべきか。これは、著作権や倫理の問題、アーティストに及ぼす経済的影響などといったさまざまな視点から論争を引き起こしている。また、これはアートの分野に限った話ではない。AIを積極的に活用しようとする意見と疑問視する考え方、双方の見解についてより深く知るには以下の文献がおすすめである。

 AI Art: Machine Visions and Warped Dreams
by Joanna Zylinska, Open Humanities Press CIC, 2020
視覚的スタイルの移行やアルゴリズム等の実験から検証し、本書はAIアートの作品が非人間的であると結論づける。また、AIのクリエイティブな分野での可能性を追求するには、美学の領域だけに閉じこもるべきではないと主張し、今日の芸術制作と創造性の状況について疑問を投げかける。

The False Promise of ChatGPT
www.nytimes.com/2023/03/08/opinion/noam-chomsky-chatgpt-ai.html
by Noam Chomsky, The New York Times, March 8, 2023
「現代言語学の父」、ノーム・チョムスキーがニューヨーク・タイムズに寄稿したChatGPTなどの生成AIに関する記事。これらに対する過大な評価や期待に警鐘を鳴らすとともに、生成AIを「擬似科学（pseudoscience）である」と断罪した。

Chapter 15

Challenges to "Forever Chemicals"

The New York Times

Humans have been changing their environment for thousands of years. Recently, the threats to our environment have become overwhelming. Can we rely on scientific innovations to save us?

Vocabulary Sorting

次の語句をカテゴリーに分類しましょう。未知語はペアで意味を確認しましょう。

contaminated water	flourine	fall apart	decay
break down	liver damage	release	dump
carbon	pry off	pollution	enzyme
oxygen	emit		

Chemical substance	Physical / Environmental harm	Divide / Split	Let go
•	•	•	•
•	•	•	•
•	•	•	•
•	•		

Words in Context

日本語のヒントを参考に、上の語句から適切な表現を選び、必要な場合は文に合うように形を変えて空欄に記入しましょう。　◎ CD3-26

In our modern industry, our fragile ecosystem is falling apart. **1.** _____ dioxide (炭素) **2.** _____ (排出) have caused serious global warming. Plastic waste, another problem, contaminates the air we breathe and the water we drink. Even worse, it is difficult to stop the **3.** _____ (汚染). However, there is hope of some solutions, such as plastic-eating **4.** _____ (酵素) that can **5.** _____ (分解する) waste rapidly or a remarkable discovery to clean the **6.** _____ (汚染水) and soil.

Reading the Article

 CD3-27

Forever chemicals no more? PFAS are destroyed with new technique

1 A team of scientists has found a cheap, effective way to destroy so-called forever chemicals, a group of compounds that pose a global threat to human health. The chemicals — known as PFAS, or per- and polyfluoroalkyl substances — are found in a spectrum of products and contaminate water and soil around the world. Left on their own, they are
5 remarkably durable, remaining dangerous for generations.

2 Scientists have been searching for ways to destroy them for years. In a study, published Thursday in the journal *Science*, a team of researchers rendered PFAS molecules harmless by mixing them with two inexpensive compounds at a low boil. In a matter of hours, the PFAS molecules fell apart.

10 **3** The new technique might provide a way to destroy PFAS chemicals once they've been pulled out of contaminated water or soil. But William Dichtel, a chemist at Northwestern University and a co-author of the study, said that a lot of effort lay ahead to make it work outside the confines of a lab.

4 Chemists first created PFAS compounds in the 1930s, and the chemicals soon proved
15 to be remarkably good at repelling water and grease. The American company 3M used
PFAS chemicals to create Scotchgard, which protects fabric and carpets. PFAS chemicals
put the nonstick in nonstick Teflon pans. Firefighters began putting out fires with
PFAS-laced foam. It's easy to encounter PFAS in our everyday lives, including in the dental
floss we thread between our teeth and the food wrappers used in restaurants.

20 **5** They're also harmful. Even low chronic levels of PFAS exposure have been linked
to an increased risk of cancer, liver damage, low birth weight and reduced immunity.
"Nearly every American has them in their bodies," said Tasha Stoiber, a senior scientist at
Environmental Working Group, an environmental advocacy group that conducts research
on PFAS chemicals.

25 **6** Handling a PFAS-laced food wrapper or wearing a pair of jeans treated with the
chemicals can expose people to their dangers. But PFAS chemicals can also reach us
through the environment. They are released into the air from factories that use them in
manufacturing. Some companies have dumped PFAS chemicals, which have spread into
rivers and groundwater. The Department of Defense has sprayed PFAS chemicals on its
30 bases during firefighting training exercises.

7 Once PFAS chemicals escape into the environment, they are pretty much there for
good because their molecular structure lets them resist decay. Each molecule is a long
carbon chain studded with fluorine atoms. The bonds between the carbon and fluorine
are so strong that they can't be broken by water, enzymes from bacteria or other natural
35 substances.

8 As a result, PFAS chemicals have accumulated in water and soil across the planet. Earlier
this month, a team of scientists reported that they could even find PFAS in raindrops falling
on Tibet and Antarctica. Many of the samples they analyzed had PFAS concentrations
higher than the level the U.S. Environmental Protection Agency considers safe. "We've
40 really polluted the whole world with this stuff," Dr. Dichtel said.

9 A crucial step in undoing the damage of PFAS chemicals is removing them from the
environment. Dr. Dichtel has been a part of this effort, inventing sticky polymers that
can pull the molecules out of contaminated water. But on its own, filtering out PFAS is
not a complete solution. "Most technologies for PFAS treatment in use today only serve
45 to remove PFAS from water, but that just concentrates the PFAS wastes," said Timothy
Strathmann, an environmental engineer at the Colorado School of Mines.

10 A common method to get rid of this concentrated PFAS is to burn it. But some studies indicate that incineration fails to destroy all of the chemicals and lofts the surviving pollution into the air. In May, the Defense Department halted its incineration of fire-suppressing foam.

11 Chemists have been searching for safer ways to get rid of PFAS, but it's been difficult to find methods that are cheap and safe. In 2020, Dr. Dichtel stumbled across a possible treatment that was surprisingly simple.

12 At the end of a PFAS molecule's carbon-fluorine chain, it is capped by a cluster of other atoms. Many types of PFAS molecules have heads made of a carbon atom connected to a pair of oxygen atoms, for example.

13 Dr. Dichtel came across a study in which chemists at the University of Alberta found an easy way to pry carbon-oxygen heads off other chains. He suggested to his graduate student, Brittany Trang, that she give it a try on PFAS molecules.

14 Dr. Trang was skeptical. She had tried to pry off carbon-oxygen heads from PFAS molecules for months without any luck. According to the Alberta recipe, all she'd need to do was mix PFAS with a common solvent called dimethyl sulfoxide, or DMSO, and bring it to a boil. "I didn't want to try it initially because I thought it was too simple," Dr. Trang said. "If this happens, people would have known this already." An older grad student advised her to give it a shot. To her surprise, the carbon-oxygen head fell off.

15 It appears that DMSO makes the head fragile by altering the electric field around the PFAS molecule, and without the head, the bonds between the carbon atoms and the fluorine atoms become weak as well.

16 Dr. Trang started testing a number of chemicals until she found one that worked. It was sodium hydroxide, the chemical in lye. When she heated the mixture to temperatures between about 175 degrees to 250 degrees Fahrenheit, most of the PFAS molecules broke down in a matter of hours. Within days, the remaining fluorine-bearing byproducts broke down into harmless molecules as well.

17 Dr. Trang and Dr. Dichtel teamed up with other chemists at U.C.L.A. and in China to figure out what was happening. The sodium hydroxide hastens the destruction of the PFAS molecules by eagerly bonding with the fragments as they fall apart. The fluorine atoms lose their link to the carbon atoms, becoming harmless. "Once you give it a chance, this thing will unzip," Dr. Dichtel said.

🔘 CD3-30

18 Dr. Dichtel and his colleagues are now investigating how to scale up their method
80 to handle large amounts of PFAS chemicals. They're also looking at other types of PFAS
molecules with different heads to see if they can pry those off as well. "It's a huge challenge,
but it's in our grasp," he said.

19 "This research is desperately needed," Dr. Stoiber said. But she cautioned that even if
the new technique works outside the lab, it will not solve the PFAS problem all by itself
85 because the scale of the problem has gotten so big — and is getting bigger.

20 Scientists estimate that over 50,000 tons of PFAS are emitted into the atmosphere each
year. Meanwhile, chemical companies are inventing new PFAS molecules at a brisk clip.
"The reality of the situation is that there is really no magic solution right now other than
undertaking the hard work of recognizing just how difficult the problem is and turning off
90 the tap so that we don't make it any worse," she said.

1,167 words

By Carl Zimmer, Aug. 18, 2022, The New York Times

Notes

ℓ.3　PFAS「ピーファス（パーフルオロアルキルおよびポリフルオロアルキル物質の略称）」:
4,730種を超える有機フッ素化合物の総称。本文にもあるように有害なだけでなく、分解しにくい
ことから「永遠の化学物質（forever chemicals）」の異名を持つ。現在は世界各国で使用が禁止・
制限されていて、日本でも沖縄や東京の多摩地域などでの（米軍基地由来とされる）PFAS汚染
が問題にされるようになり、PFOS（ペルフルオロオクタンスルホン酸）は2010年に、PFOA（ペル
フルオロオクタン酸）は2021年に製造と輸入が原則禁止された。

ℓ.15　3M「スリーエム」:
アメリカ・ミネソタ州に本拠地を置く化学・電気素材メーカー。1947年にPFOAを開発し、水と油
をはじくフッ素樹脂（テフロン）加工を世界に普及させた。PFASの有害性が懸念され始めたの
は1980年代に入ってからだが、同社は1960年代から有害性を確認していたことがのちに判明した。
同社は2022年に、2025年末までにすべてのPFAS製造の中止を表明している。

ℓ.16　Scotchgard「スコッチガード」:
3M社の防水スプレー商品。1953年に発売開始。3Mの本拠があるミネソタ州はこのスコッチガー
ドに含まれていたPFASによって州内の水道水が汚染されたとして2010年に訴訟を起こした結果、
同社は8億5,000万ドル（約900億円）を同州に支払うことで和解した。

ℓ.39　the U.S. Environmental Protection Agency（EPA）「アメリカ合衆国環境保護庁」:
国内の健康管理と自然環境の保護を管轄する米連邦政府の行政機関。EPAでは2023年に世界
で初めて飲料水に含まれるPFASの国家統一基準案を発表した。この案では飲料水1ℓに含まれ
るPFOS/PFOAそれぞれの基準値を4ng（1ng＝1gの10億分の1）とした（ちなみに日本では2023
年7月現在、環境省の"目標値"として水1ℓあたりのPFOS/PFOAの合計が50ng以下が目安）。

True or **F**alse | 英文を読んで、本文と合致する場合は T を、合致しない場合は F を記入しましょう。

1. Scientists have been trying to find an effective way to destroy PFAS for years. [ ]

2. With their strong water- and oil-repellent qualities, PFAS came to be used widely in various products. [ ]

3. PFAS do not decompose by themselves because the strong bond between carbon and fluorine in the molecules cannot be broken by natural substances. [ ]

4. Scientists recently found PFAS chemicals in the soil in Tibet. [ ]

5. Burning concentrated PFAS removed from waste destroys all harmful chemicals. [ ]

Question & **A**nswer | 次の質問に英文で答えましょう。

1. How do PFAS harm our body?

_____

2. What method did Dr. Trang try to pry off carbon-oxygen heads from PFAS molecules?

_____

3. Why does Dr. Stoiber think the research result will not solve all the PFAS problems?

_____

Correction & **L**istening | 以下は5箇所の文法上の誤りを含んだ記事の要約文です。誤りを正しく直しましょう。その後、正しい音声を聞いて答えを確認しましょう。

 CD3-31

PFAS are used in a variety of commonly used items, including Teflon pans, dental floss, and food wrappers. They are ubiquitous and are known to "forever chemicals" because they stay in the air and water for a long time. Unfortunate, these chemicals are dangerous not only to the environment, but also to our healthy. Recently, scientists have learn how to destroy PFAS. It was a remarkable discovery because it was so simple. However, the scale of the problem is so huge that it cannot easily be resolved. We are still release PFAS in enormous quantities.

Reflecting on the Whole Article

近年日本各地でも検出され大きく報道されるようになったPFAS。本記事では、有害なこの「永遠の化学物質」を除去すべく格闘する科学者たちの様子が（偶然に解決法を見つけるまでの経緯も含めて）臨場感をもってわかりやすく説明されている。解決へのトビラは開くも、先には課題が山積みである。

以下は記事全体の流れと、キーとなる英文です。ペアまたはグループを作り、これらの英文を読んで感じたことをシェアしましょう。その後、各メンバーで分担して次の質問について考え、答えを発表し合いましょう。

Paragraphs 1 – 3

PFASの除去に成功——科学誌における衝撃の発表

A team of scientists has found a cheap, effective way to destroy so-called forever chemicals, ...

Q PFAS are commonly known as "forever chemicals." Why are they named like this?

Paragraphs 4 – 8

PFASの功と罪——日常生活への普及と、人体への深刻な影

"We've really polluted the whole world with this stuff" (Dr. William Dichtel)

Q How far has PFAS pollution spread through the world?

Paragraphs 9 – 17

PFAS除去へ向けた科学者たちの格闘、偶然開いた解決へのトビラ

"I didn't want to try it initially because I thought it was too simple" (Dr. Brittany Trang)

Q Why do you think she felt this way?

Paragraphs 18 – 20

実用化へ向けたさらなる研究と残された課題

"... there is really no magic solution right now other than undertaking the hard work of recognizing just how difficult the problem is and turning off the tap so that we don't make it any worse" (Dr. Tasha Stoiber)

Q What does Dr. Stoiber mean by this statement?

Discussing the Issues

これまで不可能といわれた PFAS の分解方法が見つかったことは大きな話題となったが、今後の動向にも注意する必要がある。以下は、本章の記事に寄せられたコメントである。

 Posting Your **C**omment 次のコメントを参考に、あなた自身の意見を書いてみましょう。

Chemistry student, *4 hours ago*
It's good that Dr. Trang ended up trying the new method despite her initial skepticism. I'd like to keep up with the news about PFAS in the hope that the research results can be applied.

Romeo Lopez, *1 hour ago*
The only way that PFAS can be removed from the planet is through coordinated international action, like the Paris Agreement to combat climate change. We need to see governments around the world getting more serious.

Pessimist, *15 minutes ago*
Even if all existing PFAS were banned internationally, chemical manufacturers would probably produce new PFAS-like substances. It seems endless... what do you think?

You, *now*

_____

_____

_____

 Window to Further Research
深刻な環境問題の要因のひとつである PFAS について、日本では比較的情報量が少ないが、国内でも各所で環境被害が報告され、問題が表面化しつつある。国内外の PFAS についてさらに学び、環境問題を深く掘り下げるのに以下の本がおすすめである。

 Perfluoroalkyl Substances in the Environment: Theory, Practice, and Innovation
Edited by David M. Kempisty, Yun Xing, LeeAnn Racz, CRC Press, 2018
PFAS の歴史的な用途や化学的特性に触れ、どのように環境に影響しているかを解明。さまざまな実践的な修復技術について言及している。

 『永遠の化学物質 水の PFAS 汚染』
ジョン・ミッチェル・小泉昭夫・島袋夏子著、(阿部小涼訳)岩波書店、2020
「永遠の化学物質」である PFAS は米軍基地や工場から流出され、日本各地の水質汚染が進み、健康被害が懸念されている。本書は PFAS の歴史としくみ、日本の汚染状況と対策などを分かりやすく解説している。

Acknowledgements

Text Credits

Chapter 1   No Phones, No Apps, No Likes
From The New York Times. © [2022] The New York Times Company. All rights reserved. Used under license.

Chapter 2   Disappearing Languages
Used with permission from Nina Strochlic.

Chapter 3   Can We Communicate with Animals?
Used with permission from Condé Nast Publications.

Chapter 4   Escape from Burnout
From The New York Times. © [2022] The New York Times Company. All rights reserved. Used under license.

Chapter 5   Bringing Middle Eastern Beer to New York
From The Washington Post. © [2023] The Washington Post. All rights reserved. Used under license.

Chapter 6   The Runner Who Took a Stand
Used with permission from Guardian News & Media Limited.

Chapter 7   Reshaping the Values of Beauty
Used with permission from Guardian News & Media Limited.

Chapter 8   A Social Media Minefield: Hijab Removal Case in School
From The Washington Post. © [2023] The Washington Post. All rights reserved. Used under license.

Chapter 9   A Boy's Selfless Wish
From The Washington Post. © [2021] The Washington Post. All rights reserved. Used under license.

本書にはCD（別売）があります

Stories of the World We Live In
Unpacking Global Issues from Leading Newspapers

クオリティペーパーで読む私たちが生きる世界

2024年1月20日　初版第1刷発行
2024年3月20日　初版第3刷発行

編著者　　堀　江　恭　子
　　　　　呉　　　春　美
　　　　　Geoffrey Tozer

発行者　　福　岡　正　人
発行所　　株式会社　金　星　堂

（〒101-0051）　東京都千代田区神田神保町 3-21
　　　Tel　　（03）3263-3828（営業部）
　　　　　　（03）3263-3997（編集部）
　　　Fax　　（03）3263-0716
　　　https://www.kinsei-do.co.jp

ISBN978-4-7647-4198-0　C1082